Benchmarking in Higher Education:
Adapting Best Practices To Improve Quality

by Jeffrey W. Alstete

ASHE-ERIC Higher Education Report No. 5, 1995

Prepared by

Clearinghouse on Higher Education
The George Washington University

In cooperation with

Association for the Study
of Higher Education

Published by

Graduate School of Education and Human Development
The George Washington University

Jonathan D. Fife, Series Editor

Cite as

Alstete, Jeffrey W. 1995. Benchmarking in Higher Education. ASHE-ERIC Higher Education Report No. 5. Washington, D.C.: The George Washington University Graduate School of Education and Human Development.

Library of Congress Catalog Card Number 96-78397
ISSN 0884-0040
ISBN 1-878380-69-9

Managing Editor: Lynne J. Scott
Manuscript Editor: Sandra Selva
Cover Design by Michael David Brown, Rockville, Maryland

Publication Date: 1996

The ERIC Clearinghouse on Higher Education invites individuals to submit proposals for writing monographs for the *ASHE-ERIC Higher Education Report* series. Proposals must include:

1. A detailed manuscript proposal of not more than five pages.
2. A chapter-by-chapter outline.
3. A 75-word summary to be used by several review committees for the initial screening and rating of each proposal.
4. A vita and a writing sample.

ERIC Clearinghouse on Higher Education
Graduate School of Education and Human Development
The George Washington University
One Dupont Circle, Suite 630
Washington, DC 20036-1183

This publication was prepared partially with funding from the Office of Education Research and Improvement, U.S. Department of Education, under contract no. ED RR-93-002008. The opinions expressed in this report do not necessarily reflect the positions or policies of OERI or the Department.

EXECUTIVE SUMMARY

Increasing competition, demands for accountability, and higher volumes of available information are changing the methods of how institutions of higher education operate in the mid-1990s. For higher education to enact substantial and sustainable changes in efficiency and productivity, a new way of thinking, or paradigm, that builds efficiency and a desire for continual learning must be integrated into institutional structures. Tools are also being developed that measure, or benchmark, the progress and success of these efforts (Keeton & Mayo-Wells 1994). Among the improvement strategies and techniques such as Total Quality Management (TQM), Continuous Quality Improvement (CQI), and Business Process Reengineering (BPR), benchmarking has emerged as a useful, easily understood, and effective tool for staying competitive.

What Is Benchmarking?

Although the use of comparative data has been used for years in some industries, including higher education, benchmarking, as defined today, was developed in the early 1980s at the Xerox Corporation in response to increased competition and a rapidly declining market share (Camp 1989). The strategy of benchmarking is important both conceptually and practically. It is being used for improving administrative processes as well as instructional models at colleges and universities, by examining processes and models at other schools and adapting their techniques and approaches (Chaffee & Sherr 1992; Clark 1993). More concisely, benchmarking is an ongoing, systematic process for measuring and comparing the work processes of one organization to those of another, by bringing an external focus to internal activities, functions, or operations (Kempner 1993). The goal of benchmarking is to provide key personnel, in charge of processes, with an external standard for measuring the quality and cost of internal activities, and to help identify where opportunities for improvement may reside. Benchmarking is analogous to the human learning process, and it has been described as a method of teaching an institution how to improve (Leibfried & McNair 1992). As with other quality concepts, benchmarking should be integrated into the fundamental operations throughout the organization and be an ongoing process that analyzes the data collected longitudinally. Benchmarking attempts to answer the following questions:

- How well are we doing compared to others?
- How good do we want to be?
- Who is doing it the best?
- How do they do it?
- How can we adapt what they do to our institution?
- How can we be better than the best? (Kempner 1993)

Previously, questions like these may not have seemed important to institutions of higher education. However, in the competitive and rapidly changing markets of the 1990s (characterized by declining enrollments and funding in higher education), organizations are learning never to be satisfied with the status-quo, and to continually question their internal operations and relative position in the eyes of prospective customers. To answer these questions, several multi-step benchmarking methods have been developed by leading benchmarking practitioners (Camp 1995; Spendolini 1992; Watson 1992). Benchmarking procedures can be condensed into four steps: planning the study, conducting the research, analyzing the data, and adapting the findings to the home institution that is conducting the study. The first step involves selecting and defining the administrative or teaching process(es) to be studied, identifying how the process will be measured, and deciding which other institutions to measure against. Second, benchmarking process data is collected using primary and/or secondary research about the colleges, universities, or other organizations being studied. The third step consists of analyzing the data gathered to calculate the research findings and to develop recommendations. At this point, the differences or gaps in performance between the institutions being benchmarked help to identify the process enablers that equip the leaders in their high performance. Adaption of these enablers for improvement is the fourth step in the first iteration of a benchmarking cycle, and the primary goal of the project.

A review of the benchmarking literature shows that there are primarily four kinds of benchmarking: internal, competitive, functional/industry, and generic or best-in-class. Internal benchmarking can be conducted at large, decentralized institutions where there are several departments or units that conduct similar processes. The more common competitive benchmarking analyzes processes with peer institutions that are competing in similar markets. Functional or industry benchmarking is similar to competitive benchmarking, except that the group of competitors is larger and more broadly defined (Rush 1994). Generic or best-in-class uses the broadest application of data collection from different industries to find the best operations practices available. The selection of the benchmarking type depends on the process(es) being analyzed, the availability of data, and the available expertise at the institution.

Is Benchmarking Applicable to Higher Education?
Due to its reliance on hard data and research methodology, benchmarking is especially suited for institutions of higher education in which these types of studies are very familiar to faculty and administrators. Practitioners at colleges and universities have found that benchmarking helps overcome resistance to change, provides a structure for external evaluation, and creates new networks of communication between schools where valuable information and experiences can be shared (AACSB 1994). Benchmarking is a positive process, and provides objective measurements for baselining (setting the initial values), goal-setting, and improvement tracking, which can lead to dramatic innovations (Shafer & Coate 1992). In addition, quality strategies and reengineering efforts are both enhanced by benchmarking because it can identify areas that could benefit most from TQM and/or BPR, and make it possible to improve operations with often dramatic innovations.

Despite the majority of positive recommendations for using benchmarking and successful examples of its current use, there are critics of its applicability to higher education. The stated objections include the belief that benchmarking is merely a strategy for marginally improving existing processes, is applicable only to administrative processes (or only to teaching practices), is a euphemism for copying, is lacking innovation, or that it can expose institutional weaknesses (Brigham 1995; Dale 1995). These concerns are largely unfounded because benchmarking can radically change processes (if warranted), apply to both administration and teaching, adapt—not "adopt"—best practices, and if the Benchmarking Code of Conduct is followed, confidentiality concerns can be reduced. The Code of Conduct calls for benchmarking practitioners to abide by stated principles of legality, exchange, and confidentiality (APQC 1993). Benchmarking can make it possible for the industry to improve processes in a "leapfrog" fashion by identifying and bringing home best practices, and therefore offering a way of responding to demands for cost containment and enhanced service quality in a cost-effective and quality-oriented manner (APQC 1993; Shafer & Coate 1992).

Where Is Benchmarking Being Used in Higher Education?

Graduate business schools, professional associations such as NACUBO and ACHE, independent data sharing consortia, private consulting companies, and individual institutions are all conducting benchmarking projects. The broad-based NACUBO benchmarking program was begun in late 1991, and it seeks to provide participants with an objective basis for improved operational performance by offering a "pointer" to the best practices of other organizations. Today, nearly 282 institutions have participated in the study, and the current project analyzes 26 core functions at colleges and universities, such as accounting, admissions, development, payroll, purchasing, student housing, and others (NACUBO 1995). The Association for Continuing Higher Education (ACHE) and graduate business schools have also conducted specialized benchmarking studies that focus on the processes and practices concerning their particular institutional departments (AACSB 1994; Alstete 1996). A review of the literature finds independent benchmarking projects are currently in use, or have recently been conducted, by a wide range of institutions, such as the University of Chicago, Oregon State University, Pennsylvania State University, Babson College, and many others. These independent projects cover undergraduate and graduate teaching processes, as well as academic and business administrative practices.

How Can an Institution Get Started?

Before beginning a benchmarking study, an institution should decide if benchmarking is the correct quality improvement tool for the situation. After processes are selected for analysis, the appropriate personnel, who have a working knowledge of the area undergoing the benchmarking analysis, should then be chosen to conduct the study. A college and university can take part in an externally sponsored benchmarking project with predefined objectives, or conduct a project on its own, or with the help of consultants. It is recommended that, as a start, an institution new to benchmarking, begin with a more "grassroots" level departmental or administrative project that measures best practices internally, or with local competitors. An institution that is more advanced in quality improvement efforts can seek out world-class competitors better and implement the findings more readily than a benchmarking novice (Marchese 1995b). Information on prospective benchmarking partners can be obtained from libraries, professional associations, personal contacts, and data sharing consortia. Once the benchmarking data is collected and analyzed, it can be distributed in a benchmarking report internally within the institution and externally to benchmarking partners for implementation of improved processes. The overall goal is the adaption of the process enablers at the home institution to achieve effective quality improvement. Benchmarking is more than just gathering data. It involves adapting a new approach of continually questioning how processes are performed, seeking out best practices, and implementing new models of operation.

CONTENTS

FOREWORD

In many different ways, American higher education has been practicing benchmarking almost from the start. Harvard and the early colonial colleges were an adaptation of the English undergraduate colleges. They were an adaptation in the respect that they were not a carbon copy of the English model since the colonial colleges adjusted their curriculum, organization, and financing to meet the unique needs of early American life. When Johns Hopkins University was established, modeled on the German university, it quickly made several fundamental changes, including adding an English model undergraduate program. Later on, as new colleges were being established in the early 1800s in the Midwest, they benchmarked themselves against more established American colleges. A common refrain was that "this college will be the Harvard of...."

The essence of modeling oneself against certain standards or processes in order to produce a desired result is what benchmarking is all about. There are a number of conditions in operation today that make the process of benchmarking not only acceptable but almost mandatory for higher education. First, because of the sophistication of consumers (students, parents, employers) and sponsors (state legislators and private sponsors) of higher education, institutions are being held to a higher standard of performance. Second, not only is the knowledge base of many areas in higher education changing rapidly, awareness concerning these changes is so widespread that the stakeholders of higher education are increasingly dissatisfied with the status quo. Third, the legitimacy of new ideas based on its origin — our institution is so unique that if an idea was not developed by one of us, it could not possibly be useful — is giving way to the legitimacy based on results. If we can get our results more effectively by doing it a different way, we should change. A fourth condition, possibly a result of the other three, is a realization that through benchmarking, not only can time, energy, and money be saved, an institution can also maintain a continuous competitive edge and enhance their national reputation.

Generally speaking, benchmarking is the process of identifying someone or some organization that is doing something better than you are doing, studying how they are doing it, and adapting those procedures that would be most useful to reach your desired outcome. Benchmarking can be used to evaluate and improve specific practices (such as developing active learning in the classroom, creating more effective slide presentations, or designing a more understandable tuition and fee invoice form); better processes (establishing better ways to advise students on their academic programs or more effective ways to handle student applications); or systems, (e.g., increasing more effective use of courses over several academic programs); or creating a management enrollment system that works with students from the first contact through graduation. While benchmarking can be used successfully for any of these purposes, the greatest impact on the institution is the benchmarking of systems.

In this report by Jeffrey W. Alstete, associate dean in the Hagan School of Business at Iona College, the concept and process of benchmarking is examined with four forms of benchmarking being highlighted — internal, competitive, functional, and generic. Dr. Alstete details the specific steps that an institution needs to take in order to implement the benchmarking process and gives examples of benchmarking projects that institutions could follow.

Benchmarking in the future may not be optional. Increasingly, institutions are being asked to give specific evidence concerning the value of their outcomes as compared with other institutions. When benchmarking is carefully used to help institutions improve their processes and systems in order to better achieve their educational mission, institutions are equipped to defend against external goals and standards that could be dysfunctional and even destructive to an institution. This report will help institutions begin developing a benchmarking process that will help them to become more proactive in setting standards for their future.

Jonathan D. Fife
Series Editor,
Professor of Higher Education Administration and
Director, ERIC Clearinghouse on Higher Education

ACKNOWLEDGMENTS

I want to thank Sister Patricia Ann Reilly for her meticulous reading of my manuscript and kind recommendations. I would also like to thank Dr. Nicholas J. Beutell for his encouragement and Dr. Joseph Stetar for his guidance and suggestions. With a special thanks to my wife, Marta, for her support, I dedicate this book to her and my daughter, Jessica.

ANOTHER PART OF THE "NEW PARADIGM"

Laurence Veysey, in writing about the history of great changes that occurred in higher education during the latter part of the 19th century, stated that the American university of 1900 was all but unrecognizable in comparison with the college of 1860 (Veysey 1965). Philosophically, intellectually, and functionally, higher education had changed due to the changing needs of society. The next great period of change began after the Second World War, when the G.I. Bill of Rights made a college education more accessible to an increasingly egalitarian society, and fueled a tremendous growth in demand for higher education (Breedin 1994). As we examine institutions of higher education today, many people believe that we are at a comparable turning point or period of transition (Apps 1988; Boyer 1990). Future historians may record this transitional period as comparable to the changes that occurred in the late 1800s or from the 1950s to the 1970s. The changes that are shaping the future of higher education are due to many factors, including competition between colleges and universities and with other providers, new information technology, changes in student enrollments, financial and economic conditions, and changing societal demands. In the past, most institutions of higher education, which have adapted to the changing times, have learned new methods of operations in order to survive.

In the past, most institutions of higher education, which have adapted to the changing times, have learned new methods of operations in order to survive.

Colleges and universities are places in which learning is the main activity for students, faculty, and the administration. Personnel in higher education can be viewed as developers, brokers, and users of information, who strive to obtain and transmit the best data possible. Over the last two decades, credible authors have claimed that society is moving from an industrial age to an informational age. Vast amounts of information, and our access to it, will change nearly everything, especially the way learning takes place (Bell 1973; Naisbitt 1982; Toffler 1980). Higher education is a major source of new information through the research conducted and through the primary method of distribution —its instructional programs. However, processing tremendous volumes of information has its problems, as well as rewards. The book titled *The Coming of Post-Industrial Society* accurately predicted many of the current problems 23 years later. Bell (1973) stated:

The post-industrial society is an information society, as

industrial society is a goods-producing society. However, the centrality of information creates some new, and different problems for society to manage. These are:

1. *The sheer amount of information that one has to absorb because of the expansion of the different arenas—economic, political, and social—of men's attention and involvement . . .*
2. *The information becomes more technical . . .*
3. *There is a greater need for mediation, or journalistic translation . . . that explain the new theories to intermediate and mass audiences . . .*
4. *The sheer limits of the amount of information one can absorb . . .*
5. *Inevitably a complex society, like the large, complex organizations within it, becomes a planning society* (pp. 467-470).

The goal of this report is to address these problems, forecasted so accurately by Bell as they relate to the data and systems comparisons techniques, referred to as benchmarking, that are used by institutions of higher education to provide information for quality improvement. It is difficult today to read an academic magazine, newspaper, or education journal without coming upon an example of one of the many quality improvement methods such as Total Quality Management (TQM) or Continuous Quality Improvement (CQI), Business Process Reengineering (BPR), benchmarking, and others. These tools and the information they provide seem increasingly technical, and often use language that is unfamiliar to some readers. It is therefore appreciated, and often required, that a "mediation" or "translation" (Bell 1973) be written to help those in a specific field, such as higher education, to understand more thoroughly and possibly to utilize this new, complicated, technical information.

Among other things, this information is needed for planning. For managers in business and industry, as well as for college administrators and faculty, planning is probably the most important function. Unfortunately, much of the literature on planning is normative and consists primarily of how planning "should be done," rather than describing how planning "is done" (Sork & Caffarella 1990). These writings are often accompanied by elaborate reasons as to why the planning method should be used, but are usually lacking good examples of how it is being used effectively in organizations. This report will describe the benchmarking process, discuss examples of its use in higher education, and show how it can be used in successful planning for process improvement by the reader.

New Demands on Higher Education

Business corporations and the post-secondary educational community are both experiencing new demands emanating from the changing needs of society. Greater competition, reduced public funding, and possible financial disaster are now situations that many institutions of higher education are trying to avert as the enrollment boom from the 1960s to the 1980s subsides in the 1990s (Clotfelter, Ehrenberg, Getz & Siegfried 1991). Administrators and faculty must now address budget gaps caused by the changing demands, constricting resources, national and regional recessions, and the basic questions about the value of higher education to prospective students. In addition, while the earnings bonus attached to obtaining a college education has continued to show improvements over time, it is difficult to forecast with confidence what the returns on investments in higher education will be in the near future. These factors have had a combined impact on the financial health of many colleges and universities. When faced with reduced revenues, most colleges and universities have responded by tightening budgets, deferring non-recurring expenses, and postponing the hiring of new faculty and staff (Zemsky & Massy 1995). Some institutions and campuses were unable to stay financially competitive, such as Upsala College in New Jersey and Iona College's campus in Yonkers, New York, and have recently closed (Aronow 1993; Martin 1995).

Higher education providers are now learning that they, too, must be responsive to their environment to survive, because both the number and extensiveness of environmental forces have increased greatly in recent years (Birnbaum 1988). Both the administration and faculty feel unable to take control as resources are constrained. Often, the result is more commitment and effort to keep organizational processes, services, and goals the same, or to support the status quo. Benchmarking has been introduced as one method or tool to help create a new way of thinking, or "paradigm," for higher education to make a substantial and sustainable change in efficiency (Keeton & Mayo-Wells 1994). As changes in efficiency are built into the basic structures and functioning of colleges and universities, benchmarking can be used to seek out best practices and monitor the progress and success of the changes. For example, an associate dean at Arizona State University (ASU) stated, "We say that we want to look like a leading MBA program. [This] requires that we know what leading MBA programs look like" (Wolverton 1994, p.36). To achieve this goal, ASU's business school benchmarks information on entry standards, curriculum content, faculty credentials and salaries, placement, and starting salaries for MBA program graduates.

Clark (1993) added, "University students are older, wiser, and more determined than ever to receive a meaningful education, and at the same time, improve the quality of life" (p. 2). Clark proposed using benchmarking to help satisfy these student demands by restructuring higher education, without sacrificing the special characteristics that makes each college and university unique. For these reasons, and others discussed later in this report, benchmarking is fast becoming an important quality improvement tool. Benchmarking was recently discussed at several academic conferences, including the National Conference on Continuous Quality Improvement (Reutter 1995), the American Assembly of Collegiate Schools of Business (Bateman 1994), and the Association for Institutional Research (AIR 1994). Because today's students are more demanding, and tend to "shop" competitively, benchmarking enables colleges and universities to improve by comparing performance (both administratively and academically) with comparable or peer institutions, "best-in-class," and even world-class organizations outside of higher education. In educational testing, for example, this might mean comparing student performance, not against local norms, but against a higher set of international standards (Marchese 1991). Benchmarking provides valuable information and hard data, which is needed by colleges and universities to measure productivity. George Keller (1983) stated that "competition has not been absent from American higher education in the past century . . . But competition among colleges has begun to intensify and will increase significantly in the period ahead, requiring new campus modes of operation and new surveillance procedures" (pp. 16-17). Keller accurately predicted that the competition is not only for students, but for other resources as well.

Robert Birnbaum (1992), in researching the constraints on productivity in higher education, conducted extensive interviews with 70 trustees, administrators, and faculty leaders at seven diverse institutions of varying size and classification. He found that one of the primary rational constraints on productivity improvement is the lack of availability for data related to productivity (Birnbaum 1992). Large financial resources were thought to be required for obtaining adequate data, and the history and traditions of the institutions did not support data-related decision-making. Some of the new management improvement techniques, such as benchmarking, are designed to address these problems by making the data available at a reasonable price, and by providing the techniques for carrying out improvements in tradition-bound organizations, such as colleges and universities.

Contemporary Management Strategies
In the 1980s, public concern for quality in education, primarily for the elementary and secondary schools, was brought to national attention in the report, *A Nation at Risk: The Imperative for Educational Reform* (National Commission for Excellence in Education 1983). This report stated many concerns for education, including the belief that the increased rate of competition and changing conditions of the workplace require the need for a learning society. Later in that decade, and more strongly in the 1990s, the post-secondary level also became the focus of quality improvement. TQM, BPR, CQI, downsizing, outsourcing, and other contemporary management strategies have recently become commonplace on college and university campuses (Nicklin 1995). A variety of publications on the quality movement in higher education have all examined these programs in higher education: recent books (AAHE 1994; Seymour 1994b; Seymour 1992); journal articles (Hobbs 1994; Stein 1995), newspaper articles (Nicklin 1995); conferences (Reutter 1995), as well as recent ASHE-ERIC Reports (Chaffee & Sherr 1992; Gardiner 1994; Wolverton 1994). The complete literature on the call for improvement of management processes in higher education is too extensive to list here, and it con-

tinues to grow. Some of the literature relates concerns about the appropriateness of quality strategies in higher education, but the vast majority are positive. A search of the business periodical index for the past five years (1990-1995) found that the terms "TQM" and "benchmarking" are quite popular among business researchers (see Figure 1). The same search of the ERIC national education literature database also found that these quality principles are becoming more widely used and referred to by education researchers and authors as well (see Figure 2). This data does not nec-

FIGURE 1—Business Periodical Index Search Results for "TQM" and "Benchmarking"

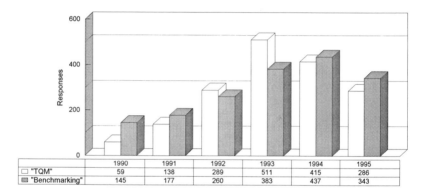

	1990	1991	1992	1993	1994	1995
□ "TQM"	59	138	289	511	415	286
▨ "Benchmarking"	145	177	260	383	437	343

FIGURE 2—Education Research Index Search for "TQM" and "Benchmarking"

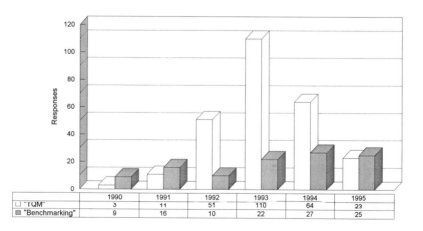

	1990	1991	1992	1993	1994	1995
□ "TQM"	3	11	51	110	64	23
▨ "Benchmarking"	9	16	10	22	27	25

essarily mean that benchmarking is being used more than TQM by colleges and universities, but its popularity trend is quite evident. The comparison between benchmarking and TQM shows that the use of competitive data to measure effectiveness, set goals, and improve processes (benchmarking) is somewhat in sequence with the more widely publicized TQM. Interestingly, TQM seems to have peaked in 1993 for both business and education periodicals, while benchmarking may have peaked in 1994 literature. In addition, other topics such as assessment (Reimann 1995; Watwood 1995), productivity (Blumenstyk 1995; Heverly & Connesky 1992) and performance indicators (Gaither, Nedwek & Neal 1994), all point toward a demand for greater efficiency and public accountability in the 1990s. Alstete (1994) and Gaither (1995) add that information technology is also helping the creation and use of these management techniques for monitoring performance and quality.

Additional evidence that the use of other quality improvement strategies may be increasing is that a recent review of 10 Boston-area colleges, which started using TQM, found that five are no longer pursuing it (Entin 1994). For the remaining institutions, the use of TQM resulted in many quality improvements.

Generally, quality efforts result in a greater customer focus, awareness of process, and new questions about outcomes and data, all of which can be taken as favorable developments for an organization. Entin (1994) stated that greater student-centeredness can happen on both the administrative and academic sides of colleges and universities. Despite higher education historian Frederick Rudolph's (1977) belief that college faculty are "suspicious of efficiency and expert at obstruction" (p. 4), administrators are not the only personnel that seek to improve the quality of higher education. Many, if not most, of the professorate also support the reform movement, and have stated that they have no quarrel with the need for changes (Bowen & Schuster 1986). The faculty not only fulfills the main functions of research, teaching, and service at colleges and universities, but they are often the first to receive student comments on the incidental and overall efficiencies of the institution. Chapter three of this report will show how benchmarking is used by both faculty and administration in higher education.

There are both vocal critics and strong proponents of

these efforts. Critics such as George Keller have stated that these projects have not been successful because "colleges and universities are ambiguous about who the customers are: students, professors, taxpayers, parents, or graduates' prospective employers" (Nicklin 1995, p. A33). In addition, some argue that colleges are using terms such as "reengineering" or "restructuring" merely as a public relations ploy to cover harsh cost-cutting and employee layoffs. Perhaps the most common complaint is that many people employed in higher education sincerely believe that colleges and universities are different from business corporations. Some institutions have responded by moderating the use of business terms and replacing them with more culturally sensitive terms, such as "committees" instead of "teams," or "indicators" instead of "measures" (Gaither et al. 1994).

However, the proponents of quality and related efforts for higher education are many, and often, they stridently stated that it can work here, too. Sherr and Lozier (1991) wrote:

If you think that these ideas make sense for industry, but that higher education is different, be assured that many corporate leaders have responded in like fashion: "But we are different." Higher education is different, and our conservativeness does make it difficult. But consider the values that TQM espouses . . . Importance of people . . . Need to Use Knowledge . . . Continuous Improvement . . . We in higher education hold dearly such values . . . (p. 10).

These sentiments are echoed by others, including Heverly and Cornesky (1992) who stated that "TQM offers a philosophy that drives everyone in the organization to use data, and it provides methods and tools for achieving this purpose" (p. 113). One of the tools referred to here is benchmarking, which we shall see is only one part of an overall quality improvement effort at a successful organization.

In reviewing the efforts of higher education and its use of TQM and restructuring strategies, Rhoades (1995) stated that these efforts often build on existing organizational structures and on past patterns of production and resource allocation. He added:

The preeminent danger is that the future of our institu-

*tions will be compromised if we simply seek continuity
with past structures; fail to restructure, rethink, and
change substantially our production processes; and do
not reallocate our work efforts to reposition ourselves in
relation to other higher education institutions, gain
public support, and increase our productivity,
resources, and quality* (p. 29).

One institution that has been a pioneer in applying total
quality management, Business Process Reengineering, and
benchmarking is Oregon State University (Shafer & Coate
1992). OSU began implementing total quality management
in 1989, and shortly thereafter achieved some process
improvement, elimination of waste in time and materials, and
cost reductions. However, in 1991, a quicker response was
demanded by the Oregon State Legislature for improved
administrative costs and support services. Benchmarking was
used as a key instrument, along with TQM and Reengineering, to ensure that improvement initiatives focus on areas
with potential for enhancement. Further, it is described in
Chapter Three how OSU used benchmarking as a continuous
process to measure its services against the competition.

Benchmarking Benefits

Benchmarking may find more of a home in higher education
than the other recently adapted management improvement
techniques, due to its reliance on research methodology and
hard data. Broadly, benchmarking is defined as "a continuous, systematic process for evaluating the products, services,
and work processes of organizations that are recognized as
representing best practices for the purpose of organizational
improvement" (Spendolini 1992, p. 9). The process in this
definition involves conducting research on competing and
noncompeting organizations which are leaders in certain
areas. Many of the research techniques used here are very
familiar to the academic community—primary and
secondary research, mail-out surveys, interviews, and others—are used for data collection and analyses. In addition,
benchmarking does not rely on purely subjective opinions
but on data collection and analysis, which are difficult to
dispute. Many practitioners have learned that, before comparing the data between the institutions being benchmarked,

the practice of compiling the benchmarking information, and making it available within their own institutions, helps create an environment that encourages colleges and universities to reexamine their operations (Blumenstyk 1995; Detrick & Pica 1995).

Another reason benchmarking has great appeal is that it is viewed as a positive process that helps institutional cultures develop learning and improving as goals. Robert Camp (1992) stated the Japanese word *dantatsu,* which means "striving to be the best of the best . . . captures the essence of benchmarking that is a positive, proactive process designed to change operations in a structural fashion to achieve superior performance" (p. 3). Additionally, Camp added that institutional leaders in the United States have no such word, because they always assumed that they were the best. Perhaps they still are in higher education, particularly in graduate studies, but global competition has a way of upsetting longstanding monopolies. Xerox learned this lesson more than 15 years ago, as Robert Camp indicated in his 1989 book, *Benchmarking: The Search for Industry Best Practices That Lead to Superior Performance.* This book reports on benchmarking efforts in the United States at Xerox, which institutionalized the practice in its organization, and fully describes the 10-step benchmarking process used. Benchmarking led to fundamental changes in how Xerox manages suppliers and develops products, and it continually forces the company to look at itself externally.

Benchmarking offers the opportunity for practitioners to think "out of the box," as Michael Spendolini (1992) describes it, and to discover new ideas. Leaders and managers tend to work in their own "boxes" most of the time, where they have been successful and are comfortable. On occasion, they may look outside this box and see what the direct competition is doing, especially if there is financial or enrollment difficulties. Benchmarking, however, takes a much more systematic approach at examining competitors and looking at processes externally. The four types of benchmarking described later (internal, competitive, functional, and generic) offer the opportunity to break out of the internal box we operate in, and discover what process leaders in other industries and world leaders are doing to achieve greatness in a particular area. Figure 3 illustrates the advantages of looking "out of the box."

FIGURE 3 — Thinking "Out of the Box"
                    (Spendolini 1992, p. 23)

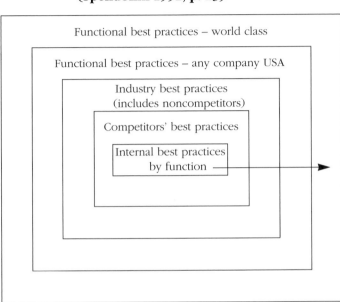

(Excerpted by permission of the publisher, from The Benchmarking Book
by Michael J. Spendolini. 1992 AMACOM, a division of the American
Management Association)

Colleges and universities are known for staying cloistered
inside the "ivory tower" and separated from the outside
world. This is due partly to our history of training clergy,
and partly to the natural barriers to change that develop in
conservative institutions, that were built to preserve and
transmit knowledge (Rudolph 1977). In today's competitive
environment, leaders in higher education must think strategi-
cally and globally to survive. In addition to gathering data
for process improvement, benchmarking is useful by college
and university leaders for strategic planning and forecasting,
because it develops knowledge of the competition, views
state of the art practices, examines trends in product/service
development, and observes patterns of customer behavior.
Benchmarking is a source for new ideas, process comparisons, and goal-setting. It enables the benchmarking practitioner to see the organizational functions from an external
point-of-view, and not be limited to the traditional method
of developing ideas and objectives internally.

Benchmarking was developed out of the dire need to improve radically; it became obvious at one organization— Xerox—that the traditional "tried and true" method of developing and producing a product was not working well because the competition had radically improved.

Initiatives at Xerox

By the early 1980s, Xerox was facing severe financial and competitive pressure. In less than a decade, Xerox's market share had fallen from more than 80 percent to about 35 percent, and the company's costs and quality were creating huge problems (Pryor 1989). In 1979, the company began a study to compare its manufacturing costs with those of foreign and domestic competitors (Camp 1992). The findings of that pioneering study showed that their competitors were selling products at a price equal to what it cost Xerox to produce them. After setting up benchmarking throughout the company, Xerox regained market share, dramatically lowered cost and improved quality, and saved itself from financial disaster.

Other industries learned to use benchmarking, too. In his follow-up book, Robert Camp (1995) wrote that, after the much publicized success of benchmarking at Xerox, other major corporations have begun successfully using benchmarking, such as Texas Instruments, Westinghouse, AT&T, IBM, and others A review of the literature found that a variety of different organizations, including many service industries, have also started using benchmarking. For example, Bergman (1994) stated that benchmarking is used in the field of health care as a management tool for improving clinical quality at Sun Health Alliance and the University Hospital Consortium. One participating hospital was able to reduce the length of stay of pneumonia patients from 8.1 to to 6.7 days, after the data was collected on patients and compared with the results from other hospitals. Benchmarking is also used on health and disability benefits in the energy and communications industries (Tortarolo & Polakoff 1995). A competitive benchmarking study of the largest 140 companies in those industries was the first project to identify the best practices and trends relating to health care and disability activities. It is clear that benchmarking has spread beyond production and warehousing operations at firms like Xerox, and on to improving performance in a wide variety of organizational and administrative processes, as well as cost concerns.

Another field that is using benchmarking, which is closely related to higher education, is employee training practices at top companies (Kimmerling 1993). The American Society for Training and Development (ASTD) has created a Benchmarking Forum, designed to be a cooperative venture among companies with strong financial and organizational commitments to employee training. Forum participants plan to find and catalog best practices by collecting information and producing comparative data against which to "peg" or benchmark their individual training efforts. The Forum began in 1991 with 19 participants, and grew to 37 in 1993. Participating companies include Aetna, American Express, Boeing, Chase Manhattan, and many others. The 1991 benchmarking findings yielded both process and financial data, including ratios of training staff to employees, training days per year, the cost of training, types of training, etc. The participants hope to measure and improve the effectiveness of the employee training. This could have an effect on colleges and universities that provide undergraduate and graduate programs, contract training, executive education, and noncredit programs for ASTD Benchmarking Forum participants.

Related to the ASTD benchmarking effort, Ford (1993) reported that benchmarking is applicable to the area of human resources/training. It has resulted in identifying the strengths and weaknesses of management's training efforts. Ford stated:

> *David Ulrich and his colleagues at the University of Michigan have already done some ground-breaking work. They conducted a large benchmarking study of human resources competencies and practices, which involved more than 10,000 individuals in 91 U.S. firms. Focusing on all HR functions, they collected surveys from managers and employees in many functional areas, measuring perceptions of the companies human resources departments.*

Among the competencies they examined were eight in the HRD domain:
- training program design
- training delivery

It is clear that benchmarking has spread . . . to improving performance in a wide variety of organizational and administrative processes, as well as cost concerns.

- career planning
- career development
- organizational design
- autonomous work-group design
- organizational restructuring
- integration of business functions (p. 38).

The first two areas in the Ulrich study, training program design and training delivery, show that corporations are not only benchmarking administrative processes and how much they spend on training, but how they train. Since companies are benchmarking processes in higher education that we would label as academic/curricular, there is evidence that our college and university academic programs should also be able to use benchmarking effectively. This has already begun in some areas of secondary education, such as technical education (Inger 1993; Losh 1994).

Inger (1993) stated that educators normally look only at other schools for practices to borrow. Successful benchmarking can be used to look both inside and outside the field of education for best practices. Because benchmarking focuses on outcomes, it can be applied to "tech prep" as an organizational alternative to the traditional secondary school college prep and general education program. Inger believes that the following components of tech prep are particularly well suited to benchmarking: articulation, program assessment and improvement, career guidance, and marketing. Many of these overlap with functions in higher education. Benchmarking has also been proposed for benchmarking technical education *delivery* systems as a method for improving vocational-technical education (Losh 1994). As a start, a tech prep consortia in Arizona are establishing metrics to benchmark a statewide system, with the initial goal of discussing and ratifying the processes to be measured by the participants.

The Baldrige Award and Benchmarking
As we have seen, calls for education to adapt strategies from business and industry are not new. Even the famous Malcolm Baldrige National Quality Award, the "icon" of corporate quality management improvement, has now been extended to higher education (Seymour 1996). The Baldrige Award was created in 1987 by President Ronald Reagan, and

is given annually to selected companies and other organizations that practice effective quality management techniques that result in significant improvements in the quality of their goods and services (Seymour 1994a). To date, more than 1 million copies of the Baldrige Criteria have been distributed, almost 300 companies have applied for the award and there have been 28 winners (Seymour 1996). Among the core values of the award is the need for management by fact, where data and data analyses support a variety of organizational purposes, including planning, assessing performance, improving the organization's structure and processes, and comparing its quality performance against the performance benchmarks of other organizations. The benchmarking process is an important part of the award criteria, which uses a rating system with 1,000 possible points that award candidates strive to achieve. The "management by fact" core value is achieved through required, competitive benchmarking in two of the 1995 pilot education criteria categories (see Appendix A). Criteria items number 2—Information and Analysis (worth 75 points) and item 6—Institutional Performance Results (worth 230 points), both require that colleges and universities conduct benchmarking studies in an ongoing manner, in order to receive the Baldrige points. The best performers in this category gather hard data to measure quality trends for key programs and services, compare quality with national averages and national leaders in comparable organizations, measure trends in overall performance of operational process and support services, and examine the quality of supplies and services furnished by other providers (Chaffee & Sherr 1992). The Baldrige office at the National Institute of Standards and Technology is working with the Academic Quality Consortium from the American Association for Higher Education "to provide campuses committed to implementing continuous quality improvement the opportunity to learn and work collaboratively by exchanging information, building on one another's experiences, and expanding on the assessment practices already being utilized" (Seymour 1996, p. xi). An excellent description of these efforts are detailed in the two-volume set, "High Performing Colleges: The Malcolm Baldrige National Quality Award as a Framework for Improving Higher Education" (Seymour 1996). The first volume covers the theory and concepts of the award, and the second volume discusses the application and implementation, as well as valid concerns of the 1995 Education Pilot award criteria at Northwest Missouri State University. Ted Marchese (1994) from the American Association for Higher Education, wrote that, "The Baldrige will work in higher education, just as [it] has (and hasn't) in industry, when it is embraced by the internal culture as a tool for improvement (p. 4). The use of benchmarking processes as part of Northwest Missouri State University's pursuit of the Baldrige Award is further described in Chapter 3 of this report. In addition, the Baldrige Award has sparked the creation of several state-level, Baldrige-type quality awards that are already being applied to higher education. For example, Rio Salado Community College received the Pioneer Award from the Arizona Quality Alliance in 1993 (Seymour 1994b). Organizations using benchmarking and applying the Baldrige Award (or Baldrige-type) criteria clearly perceive themselves as leaders in their respective markets (APQC 1993).

Summary

Much has been written about the need for change and improvement in higher education, and new paradigms, or models, of operation have been proposed to address these changes. Among them is the call for the creation of a more "learning centered," organizational structure, where the emphasis is not on traditional teaching but on what the students learn (Barr & Tagg 1995). In addition, quality improvement techniques developed in the business world such as TQM, reengineering, the Baldrige Award, and benchmarking are being used as tools in these new paradigms, or ways of thinking for colleges and universities. Benchmarking, as described in the next chapter, is part of the new paradigm, and is fundamentally about learning. It offers the opportunity to see the organization from "out of the box," and provides the methodology for a continuous process of comparing and learning for an organization. Having faced turmoil in the global marketplace, other industries have had to change the way they operate, and they have used benchmarking as part of these changes. Benchmarking was brought into the mainstream of management practices at Xerox in the early 1980s. Since then, it has been used in a variety of industries, and has become part of the lexicon of continuous quality improvement in the 1990s. The literature

of business and education shows that its popularity contin-
ues to grow, and it is now being used in many colleges and
universities.

WHAT IS BENCHMARKING?

As with many other terms, benchmarking is often used incorrectly or too broadly in regard to the true and original definition. Benchmarking does not mean comparing numbers for simply obtaining information on the performance of an organization or difference between two organizations. Government agencies, in particular, have used "benchmark" or "benchmarking" to describe a procedure of devising performance or outcome measures to calculate an agency or organization's progress toward improvement (PSQR 1994). Benchmarking is different from creating a set of performance standards; it involves continually comparing an organization's performance and learning from moving targets, by identifying the process leaders. In a recent ASHE-ERIC Report on the use of Performance Indicators in higher education, the authors commented on the difference in definition, and stated that performance indicators are useful for comparing performance and quality among peers over time, whereas benchmarks are useful for improving specific processes in an institution by comparing to peers and adapting techniques (Gaither et al. 1994).

Collaborative and cooperative learning have recently been promoted as techniques that college students can use to learn by helping each other (Bosworth & Hamilton 1994; Bruffee 1993). Since higher education is often viewed as a learning business, colleges and universities, as institutions, should also be inclined to learn from each other, and from other organizations outside higher education through the business-developed process called "benchmarking." One benchmarking program manager defined benchmarking as "The process by which organizations learn, modeled on the human learning process" (Watson 1993, p. 2). Leibfried and McNair (1992) also stated that benchmarking is analogous to the human learning process:

> *Benchmarking, then, is a class on learning how to learn. The first few lectures are simply to get your attention. Once the groundwork is laid, the pace of change accelerates, as every individual begins to accept the fact that the status quo is a dangerous bedfellow. As novel approaches to organizing internal work are uncovered and measurements are derived to support them, attitudes change. People can become accustomed to change. In fact, change can become exhila-*

rating. The final exam for the class is conducted by the market; those that embrace change and strive for constant improvement will survive in the twenty-first century. Those that remain mired in tradition will get failing marks, perhaps even flunk out of school (p. 323).

There are many other definitions of this relatively new management process but, fundamentally, benchmarking involves *analyzing performance, practices, and processes, within and between organizations and industries, to obtain information for self-improvement.* Institutions of higher education have been conducting external data gathering and comparisons for years, but benchmarking as defined here, also involves the search for best practices. Benchmarking, as defined today, may be particularly appealing to the academic community, due to its reliance on research methodology. This methodology is not unlike that practiced and taught by faculty and administrators in colleges and universities everyday. Surveys, interviews, data collection, analysis, and reporting are all techniques with which most people in higher education are very familiar. The other quality improvement techniques recently introduced to higher education often involve using unfamiliar business labels and terminology such as "customer," with which many in higher education are not entirely comfortable (Chaffee & Sherr 1992). Therefore, benchmarking offers a new way of thinking, or paradigm, that may be more acceptable to personnel in academia.

The definition of benchmarking is more focused than the other quality techniques, is easily understandable, and can be respected because it is data driven. Members of the Design Steering Committee at the American Productivity and Quality Center (APQC) developed the following definition: *Benchmarking is the process of continuously comparing and measuring an organization with business leaders anywhere in the world to gain information, which will help the organization take action to improve its performance* (APQC 1993, p. 4).

Another definition developed at the APQC represents a consensus among some 100 firms:

Benchmarking is a systematic and continuous measurement process; a process of continuously measuring

*and comparing an organization's business processes
against business process leaders anywhere in the world
to gain information, which will help the organization
take action to improve its performance* (Watson 1993,
p. 3).

The second definition adds that benchmarking should be
integrated into the ongoing operations of the institution. As
with quality efforts, it is ongoing because looking at the data
longitudinally can be beneficial in showing the progress
made by the participating organizations. A stagnant, one-
time snapshot of a process that has been benchmarked may
be interesting and even somewhat useful, but to see the
success (or failure), over time of process changes and
improvements, is much more valuable. Often, charting and
seeing the results of improvement efforts can be very useful
in motivating those who are conducting the benchmarking,
as well as to the customers of the process who will receive
the benefits of any improvements enacted.

Benchmarking Process Overview
Benchmarking's relationship with quality strategies is even
more visible as the process is further defined. The benchmarking process can be compared to the simple four-step
approach: Plan-Do-Check-Act (PDCA), as shown in Figure 4.
Chaffee and Sherr (1992) and the other literature on quality
also call PDCA the Shewart Cycle, which was the fundamental method taught by management guru, W. Edwards
Deming.

**FIGURE 4—Benchmarking Process Compared with the
Deming Cycle (Watson 1993)**

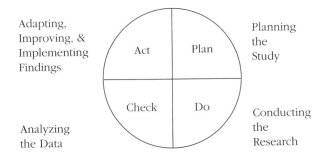

The first step in benchmarking, as in the PDCA cycle, starts with planning. For higher education, this means selecting and defining the administrative or teaching process to be studied, identifying how the process will be measured, and then deciding which institutions or organizations should be studied. In other words, it involves planning what to benchmark and who to benchmark with, if the benchmarking project will be more than an internal study (described later in this report). The second step uses primary and/or secondary research to gather the data. This can involve researching publicly available information about the target colleges and universities through professional associations, personal contacts, a library, or on-line computer services. The primary research may involve direct communication via telephone surveys, written questionnaires, or visits to make detailed inquiries. The third step in benchmarking consists of analyzing the data gathered to calculate the research findings and develop recommendations. This is the critical point in study where the differences, or gaps, between the participants performance are identified, and from which the "process enablers" are derived. Understanding and applying these enablers to the organization conducting the benchmarking study is the essence of the benchmarking process. The overall goal is improved performance from these enablers that were learned from the other organization(s) and then adapted. Watson (1993) summarized the following important point:

A benchmark study produces two results: (a) a measure of process performance excellence that can be used as a standard for comparison . . . and (b) a determination of the process enablers that helped develop the level of performance observed . . . . These enablers are the key to improving the observer company's performance, and their discovery is the real goal of the benchmarking study (p. 17).

Adaptation of these enablers for improvement is the fourth and final step in the benchmark process, at least in the first iteration of the cycle. For benchmarking to be truly effective, the process should be never ending. Organizational leaders should never believe that they can, or should, stop comparing their performance with others.

A detailed, 10-step process was defined in Camp's first book in 1989, and it is also widely used elsewhere. In his 1995 follow-up companion book, *Business Process Benchmarking*, Camp stated that different companies have diverse benchmarking models with varying numbers of steps in the benchmarking process. They have similar terminology and overlapping areas, but differing levels of process description (see Figure 5). In addition to Xerox's 10-step process, there is a nine-step process at Alcoa, a 12-step process at AT&T, and a five-step process at IBM. All of these multi-step benchmarking processes can be looked at in conjunction with the four phases of the aforementioned PDCA cycle.

The first phase involves planning the benchmarking study by deciding what organizational processes are to be benchmarked, to whom these processes will be compared, and how the data will be collected. After deciding what, who, and how the benchmarking project will be conducted, the actual data collecting is done through primary and secondary research. There is no one correct way to conduct all benchmarking studies, and the different studies require different methods of gathering the information. Recognizing that the purpose of benchmarking is not only to derive quantifiable metrics and targets, but more importantly, it is used to investigate and document the best practices that enable the achievement of the goals and targets. The second phase contains the analysis of the benchmarking data where the performance gaps between the organizations are identified, and provides the objective basis on which to improve the process. The performance gaps must then be used for adapting improvement efforts, and setting operation goals for change. The plans for change should contain markers for updating the benchmarking findings, because the external practices of the other organizations are constantly changing, or continuously improving.

Benchmarking really has two important overall components or process groups: the management of the benchmarking process and the user processes (Camp 1995). The processes described above are what the users of benchmarking do, while the managers who supervise the overall project have their own broader process steps to establish support and sustain the benchmarking effort. Figure 6 shows the relationship between the management of the benchmarking process with the step-wise user processes.

FIGURE 5—Benchmarking process models (Camp 1995, p. 9) adapted from *Comparing Process Models for Benchmarking*, **American Productivity and Quality Center**

	4-step	6-step	7-step	8-step	10-step
Planning the study	Prepare to benchmark	Plan	Determine functions or processes to benchmark Identify key performance variables Identify best-in-class companies	Define business issue Define what to benchmark Define benchmark measures Determine who to benchmark	Identify process Identify partner
Collecting process data	Research process	Research Observe	Measure performance	Acquire data	Collect data
Analyzing data for results	Document best practices	Analyze	Compare performance and estimate gaps	Compare performance Indentify actions to close the gap	Determine gap Project future performance
Adapting for improvement	Report and implement	Adapt Improve	Specify improvement programs and actions Implement and monitor results	Implement improvements and monitor results	Gain support Set goals Develop plans Implement plans Recalibrate benchmarks
Number of companies Percentage of companies	6 14%	7 17%	8 19%	4 10%	8 19%

FIGURE 6—Benchmarking processes and phases (Camp 1995, p. 10)

Management process: Establish	Support	Sustain
User process:	10-Step	

Benchmarking provides an objective measurement for base-lining, goal-setting, and improvement tracking (Detrick, Magelli & Pica 1994). It helps sort out what should be measured, and provides insight to the inefficiencies of certain processes. Benchmarking is truly a learning experience for those managers that participate. Often, during the initial stage of planning of what to benchmark and the gathering of internal data, an organization learns immediately that there are obvious inefficiencies. This often happens in the consortium or association-type benchmarking studies, where participants are first mailed a survey form to collect industry standards and then begin to fill in their own data on the form. However tempting this might be, this is not the goal, or best result possible for benchmarking. The benchmarking manager should ensure that the project team does not slow down and get too involved at the self-analysis stage.

... benchmarking can help overcome resistance to change that can be very strong in conservative organizations ...

More importantly, benchmarking can help overcome resistance to change that can be very strong in conservative organizations, such as colleges and universities, that have had little operational change in many years. It does this by relying on data and analysis, which are difficult to argue, if the data are valid and the analysis has merit. Decision-makers in higher education, that have years of training and experience in academic or business research, often welcome data-based recommendations. However, benchmarking is not an end in itself, but rather a means to an end, which is organizational improvement. *Researchers can easily get caught up in the details of data collection and analysis, and [they] should remember to keep the goal of process improvement in sight at all times.*

In *The Benchmarking Book*, Michael J. Spendolini (1992) summarizes what benchmarking is, and is not, (Table 1). As stated earlier, benchmarking is a continuous process, not a one-time event. Although it can have great benefits, even if performed successfully only once, the improvement gained can easily be lost as competitors improve their own processes. Benchmarking is not a process that provides simple answers through the numbers reported (the "metrics"), or in the process enablers that are the means for achieving the better numbers. It is a process that provides valuable information that needs to be incorporated, or adapted, into the organization that hopes to improve, and can identify industry standards. W. Edwards Deming offered the following advice on this, "Adapt, don't Adopt" (Watson 1993, p. 3). The process enablers are originally developed at the institutions that have best practices to meet their own specific needs, in their own specific environment. Since no two organizations or competitive environments (especially colleges and universities) are exactly alike, the process enablers need to be adapted to fit. Outright copying of a business process, without thorough analysis for organizational fit, can cause unforeseen problems.

TABLE 1

**Benchmarking: What it Is and Isn' t
(Spendolini 1992, p. 33).**

Benchmarking Is	Benchmarking Isn' t
A continuous process	A one-time event
A process of investigation that provides valuable information	A process of investigation that that provides simple answers
A process of learning from others; a pragmatic search for ideas	Copying, imitating
A time-consuming, labor intensive process requiring discipline	Quick and easy
A viable tool that provided useful information for improving virtually any business activity	A buzzword, a fad

(Excerpted by permission of the publisher, from The Benchmarking Book by Michael J. Spendolini. 1992 AMACOM, a division of the American Management Association)

This is why benchmarking is not as quick and easy as it first seems. Although benchmarking is not difficult, it does require sufficient planning, employee training, time, and financial support. The costs will be discussed later; however, practitioners of benchmarking in higher education report that the return-on-investment is very respectable (AACSB 1994; NACUBO 1995). Benchmarking is effective in higher education for several reasons. First, it is easy to understand and implement by all levels of employees in the organization, for all kinds of processes. Second, many companies, such as Xerox, Motorola, IBM, and others, have been using it for years (Spendolini 1992). Third, benchmarking uses reliable research techniques, such as surveys, interviews, and site visits, which provide external and objective measurements for goal-setting, and for improvement tracking over time.

Thomas J. Sergiovanni (1995), a leading writer on educational administration, commented that school administrators tend to jump at every latest management fad. This may have some truth; however, most of these adapted management strategies do have one thing in common: the key to productivity improvement lies in performing better through continuous organizational learning (Marchese 1995a), which is what benchmarking also offers. Benchmarking is clearly more than a fad. It is a learning experience for those who participate, because its method forces participants to analyze and compare continually, identify industry standards, and set the definitions for performance. Just as there are different kinds of learning that can be planned, the suitable form of benchmarking should also be chosen. The literature reviewed shows there are at least four kinds of benchmarking:

- Internal benchmarking
- Competitive benchmarking
- Functional/Industry benchmarking
- Generic benchmarking

Benchmarking can be conducted against internal operations, external direct competitors, industry functional leaders, and generic processes (Camp 1989). Each type of benchmarking has advantages and disadvantages, and some are simpler to conduct than others. The manager in charge of the benchmarking project should look at each type to determine if it is worth the cost and effort to yield the desired information. Table 2 contrasts the main advantages of each benchmarking type.

Internal and competitive benchmarking have the most relevant data to the operation being benchmarked.

Table 2

**Key Benchmarking Characteristics
(Camp 1989, p. 57)**

Benchmarking Operation	Relevance	Data Collection Ease	Innovative Practices
Internal Operations	X	X	
Direct Product Competitors	X		
Industry Leaders		X	X
Generic Processes		X	X

However, neither of these processes usually results in obtaining world-class breakthrough innovations. The other types, except for competitive benchmarking, are not hampered by obtaining sensitive information that may be confidential. However, the industry and generic processes are more difficult to benchmark, because the practitioner must decide how to adapt the best practices to the home organization, which may be in a different industry. The most significant benefit of benchmarking lies in discovering the world-class leading processes in a parallel process, usually in a different industry. This is how Xerox moved forward in the reproduction industry by competitively benchmarking warehousing and distribution processes from L. L. Bean, which is in a completely different industry.

Internal Benchmarking

Many organizations that are highly decentralized, such as colleges and universities, can take advantage of a highly cost-effective method called "internal benchmarking." This is a type of benchmarking in which processes are compared between operating units, divisions, or sister companies (Watson 1993). For institutions of higher education, this can mean different departments, or schools, within a college or university. For example, faculty hiring processes could be benchmarked between the humanities, education, and the science departments, or a graduate school of business could benchmark its graduate admissions processes with other professional graduate schools. These internal benchmarking studies can produce detailed data about process improvement opportunities, because the usual hurdles of access and cooperation from other institutions will be reduced if it is done within one college or university system. Internal studies can also help the organization focus on the critical issues to be examined, provide useful information by themselves, and define areas for future external investigations. Although it has these benefits, internal benchmarking has a lower probability of achieving significant breakthroughs, because comparable departments within one college system tend to have relatively similar practices and processes compared with external organizations.

Competitive Benchmarking

A more common type of benchmarking focuses on measuring performance against peer or competitor organizations. The goal of competitive benchmarking is to study the product designs, process capabilities, and/or administrative methods used by an organization's competitors or peers (Watson 1993). This is one of the primary goals of the association-sponsored benchmarking projects in higher education, such as the NACUBO study (National Association of College and University Business Officer), which will be described in detail later in this report. Institutions of higher education are very familiar with classifications, such as the Carnegie classification system, public versus privately-funded, small colleges versus large universities, the Ivy League, the Big Ten, etc. The participants in competitive benchmarking seek to analyze their processes directly against those organizations with whom they have similarities but on processes that may not be particularly sensitive. Watson (1995) stated:

> Studies of this type differ from process benchmarking studies in terms of their depth, and the fact that their goal tends to end with measurement, rather than with implementing process enablers. Competitive benchmarking studies may be conducted directly with competitors on benchmark processes that are noncontroversial, such as facilities management, internal auditing practices, human resource practices, employee safety and health, compensation and benefits, employee training and development, quality programs and methods, purchasing and supplier management,

and industrial policy issues. Often these studies are conducted by a third party to sanitize the competitive information, nominalize sensitive performance information to an agreed-on base measure, and report case study information that has been approved by the contributing company (p. 109).

It is easy to see why third-parties, such as professional associations like NACUBO, the Association for Continuing Higher Education (ACHE), or private consulting firms like the American Productivity and Quality Center (APQC), and Educational Benchmarking Incorporated (EBI), are popular methods by which colleges and universities enter the benchmarking field. Benchmarking practitioners often ask for a neutral and external standard for institutional comparison of processes. After internally analyzing a process and determining a benchmark, a manager typically may ask if this result is really good, and if so, compared with whom (Detrick & Pica 1995; Rush 1994). Another reason for seeking external third-party analysis for competitive benchmarking, particularly for large organizations, is that one-to-one comparisons with competitors can raise concerns over possible antitrust violations and unfair trading practices (Watson 1993). Some information may be impossible to obtain because it is proprietary, and it is the reason for an institution's competitive advantage (Camp 1989). However, while obtaining information may be not be easy, it should nevertheless be pursued, perhaps by using third party associations or consultants to guarantee confidentiality and anonymity.

Functional Benchmarking

Also called industry benchmarking, functional benchmarking is similar to competitive benchmarking, except that the group of competitors analyzed is larger and more broadly defined (Rush 1994). Robert Camp (1995) defines functional benchmarking as "a comparison of methods to companies with similar processes in the same function outside one's industry" (p.15). This kind of benchmarking presents a good opportunity to produce breakthrough results by analyzing high performing processes and learning the process enablers from these industry-wide organizations (Watson 1993).

Xerox found, through functional benchmarking, that it could look outside its industry for best practice leaders and relate it to an overall company-wide benchmarking effort. As briefly described in the first chapter of this report, Xerox realized that it needed to radically improve performance and decided to look at a warehousing and distribution process leader in another industry—L. L. Bean.

Despite their differences, the similarities between Xerox and L. L. Bean were very efficient operations, designed with the full participation of the hourly workforce, and they used quality circles to do it (Camp 1989). L. L. Bean was identified as a best practice leader in the area of warehousing and distribution through an article published in a trade periodical. Since Xerox and L. L. Bean are in two very different industries, the problem of confidentiality was reduced, and a distribution manager at L. L. Bean agreed to a site visit by Xerox personnel. The visit was conducted, and data was gathered and compared between the two organizations. L. L. Bean also learned about the benchmarking process itself and began visiting other firms (although, not Xerox) to learn from them, as well.

For colleges and universities, functional benchmarking means analyzing institutions outside of one's Carnegie classification or funding type, as well as organizations outside of the field of higher education altogether. Possible functional or industry benchmarking partners might train and educate divisions of large firms, private training companies, elementary or secondary schools, or new nontraditional, computer-based distance learning programs. Looking within a narrowly-defined competitive group of organizations has obvious limitations in a rapidly changing world. This is why functional benchmarking can be one of the most productive and cost-effective benchmarking types. The objective is for the colleges and universities to learn about competitors in a general way, rather than specifically (Thor 1995). Overall, the goal of both competitive and functional benchmarking is to identify the best operational practices and processes that can be adapted or learned from the leaders.

Generic Benchmarking

Generic benchmarking, also called "best-in-class," uses the broadest application of data collection from different kinds of organizations. Generic benchmarking compares work processes at one organization to others who have truly innovative and exemplary performance (Camp 1995). Generic benchmarking, which is also known as "best-in-class" benchmarking, Rush (1994) stated:

> . . . *seeks out those organizations with the best practices regardless of the industry. The basic criterion is: Who performs this activity best? As a result, a college or university might compare itself to an airline's purchasing process, a credit card company's billing process, or a manufacturer's facilities maintenance operation.* (p. 90)

The value of generic benchmarking is that an organization is not restricted to a competitive or industry group of institutions, and is equipped to look at important internal processes, *generally* for analogous processes elsewhere (Watson 1993). The difference between functional and generic benchmarking is that generic benchmarking seeks to uncover the "best of the best" practices, regardless of industry. The organizations doing the functional benchmarking must understand how the processes can translate across industries, and they need to look for the leaders accordingly. Therefore, generic benchmarking is probably the most difficult benchmarking type to use, but can have the highest probability for long-term returns. This creative approach can often result in changed standards and a complete reengineering of business operations. Robert Dale (1995), a benchmarking consultant to higher education, recently held a conference where he stated that reengineering is really the natural result of benchmarking. If, during a benchmarking project, it is determined that the processes under scrutiny need to be changed entirely, then complete process reengineering may be the proper tool. However, if only minor adjustments are needed, or changes are required in other areas of the organization, then reengineering may not be the tool for this job. Benchmarking and reengineering are related techniques, but they have different purposes and uses in an overall quality improvement effort.

Each of the four benchmarking types can be important tools for process analysis and quality improvement. The type that should be used depends on the kind of process being analyzed, the availability of data, and the accessibility of potential benchmarking partners for the college or university conducting the benchmarking study. Regardless of which benchmarking type is used, the purpose is still the same—to help the organization continually learn from other organizations (Camp 1995). This is done by analyzing the operation, knowing the competition and industry leaders, incorporating the best of the best, and finally gaining superiority to become the new benchmark for others to seek.

Focus and Approach
The literature on benchmarking contains different focuses and approaches to benchmarking. There are two primary kinds of focus levels: strategic benchmarking and operational-level benchmarking, and primarily two approaches to benchmarking, problem-based and process-based. In his book titled *Strategic Benchmarking*, Gregory Watson (1993) stated that strategic benchmarking is different from operational benchmarking in that it concentrates on:

- *Building core competencies that will help sustain competitive advantage.*
- *Targeting a shift in strategy such as developing new products or entering new markets.*
- *Developing a new line of business or making an acquisition.*
- *Creating an organization that is more capable of learning.* (pp. 33-34)

With a strategic focus on benchmarking, the organization looks at its overall competitive strengths and weaknesses to understand and develop competitive product and service strategies (Camp 1995). The strategic focus establishes goals for product or service performance, customer support levels, asset usage, and financial usage. It also develops the key practices needed to achieve the strategic goals. This helps the organization to take an external focus on their industry trends, overall direction, and basic product or service offerings.

In comparison, operational benchmarking is used to understand specific customer requirements and the best practices to achieve customer satisfaction by improving internal organizational processes. This is also called "functional" or "practical benchmarking," and is most useful to mid-level managers, because it enables the employees closer to the customer to become the competitor of choice.

Examples of operational benchmarking at a college or university include functional processes in offices such as purchasing, admissions, bursar, registrar, and other customer focused areas. Rush (1994) wrote a partial list of administrative areas for operational benchmarking at a hypothetical university, which is detailed in Table 3. Rush also stated that a university executive might ask, why should costs, such as processing a purchase order or an application for admission be important?

TABLE 3

Functional Benchmarks in Higher Education (Rush 1994)

Dept./Function/ Process	Customer	Output	Cost/Output	Avg. Elapsed Time
Purchasing	Faculty/Staff	Purchase Order	$26.00	11 days
Student Admissions	Prospective Student	Accept/Reject	$37.00	3 months
Registrar	Student	Grade Reports	$11.00	2 weeks
Facilities Work Order	Faculty/Student/ Staff	Completed Work Order	$18.00	4 weeks
Personnel	Faculty/Staff	Position Reclassification	$73.00	6 months
Development	Donors	Gift Acknowledgement	$19.00	6 weeks

The answer is that these are the types of processes that drive a significant portion of the costs at colleges and universities. The payroll of the personnel and the aggregate transaction costs of items, such as those stated above, can be quite large. For example, if an institution is processing 13,000 admission applications per year at a cost of $37 each, the institution will spend $481,000 on that activity each year. A 30 percent reduction in individual transaction costs would yield a savings of $144,300 per year. Operational benchmarking, although perhaps not as appealing to senior level administrators as long-term trends and goals, is nevertheless very important to organizational survival in a competitive environment.

Aside from a strategic or operational focus, benchmarking can also have either a problem or process-based approach. This involves how benchmarking is to be initialized and used in the organization. In a problem-based approach, the activity is characterized as uncontrolled, because there is no specific plan for the benchmarking effort (Camp 1995). In this approach, benchmarking is conducted on a problem-by-problem basis as organizational troubles occur. A more thoughtful approach is process-based, where benchmarking is part of an overall quality and continuous improvement effort, and should be planned for accordingly. The process-based approach can be successful in bringing order to managing benchmarking within an institution, and for high efficiency, it should be applied only to the vital few business processes. It can be inefficient and unwieldy to benchmark too many processes or only certain ones identified by noticeable problems.

Another perspective on benchmarking is that it can differ in the view it provides an institution (NACUBO 1995). Vertical benchmarking seeks to quantify the costs, workloads, and productivity of a predefined functional area, such as undergraduate admissions or accounts payable. Horizontal benchmarking measures the cost and productivity of a single process that goes across more than one functional area, such as processing a travel request or purchase order. More corporations, nonprofit organizations, and institutions of higher education are using benchmarking as the key tool for making both strategic and operational changes, on problem and process-based approaches, and horizontally or vertically within their structures.

More corporations, nonprofit organizations, and institutions of higher education are using benchmarking as the key tool for making both strategic and operational changes, on problem and process-based approaches, and horizontally or vertically within their structures.

Criticisms of Benchmarking

Despite all of the positive recommendations for benchmarking cited in this report, there are critics of the benchmarking process and its applicability to higher education. Wolverton (1994) stated that benchmarking, as a cornerstone of CQI in higher education, is based only on current information, and may not give us the freedom and flexibility to see the future. In addition, Wolverton added that this focus may relegate us to the role of follower, instead of leader. In writing about a related quality improvement technique, Business Process Reengineering (BPR), Hammer and Champy (1993) added that:

The problem with benchmarking is it can restrict the Reengineering team's thinking to the framework of what is already being done in its company's own industry. By aspiring only to be as good as the best in its industry, the [Reengineering] team sets a cap on its own ambitions. Used this way, benchmarking is just a tool for catching up, not for jumping way ahead (p. 132).

This is an important point, because many business and education writers believe that benchmarking involves only examining the same institutional sector (i.e., liberal arts colleges should only benchmark liberal arts colleges). However, we have seen that functional and generic-type benchmarking do reach across industries, and can indeed "jump way ahead." In addition, it must be remembered that benchmarking is only one of many quality improvement tools that faculty and administrators can use in different situations. Since reengineering involves "a fundamental rethinking and radical redesign of business processes to achieve dramatic improvements in critical, contemporary measures of performance . . ." (Hammer & Champy, 1993, p. 32), benchmarking may be appropriate only where the process can be improved immediately by this method, and not need a complete redesign as provided by reengineering. On the positive side, Hammer and Champy stated that benchmarking can help a reengineering team by sparking new ideas, especially if companies are benchmarked from outside their own industry.

Robert Pedersen (1992), from West Virginia University, questioned the applicability of all recent quality improvement techniques to higher education, and stated that benchmarking and TQM are merely strategies for marginally improving existing processes, which seek to bring results more closely in line with expectations. He believes that the costs of such analyses frequently outweigh any possible benefits, and lack strategic vision. Another colleague in Great Britain, David Kerridge (1995), added that the whole concept of benchmarking is foreign to the true Deming philosophy, and stated that organizations do not need to know how good they are now and how they compare with others in order to make improvements. Rebecca Christianson (1995) at Michigan Technological University, stated that benchmarking can have an impact on administrative practices, such as the registration process, but would like to see it applied to the teaching and learning processes. However, she is concerned that many faculty members seem content with the current teaching evaluation system as it stands now, and that a recently implemented fast feedback system for quality improvement is mostly perceived as a nuisance. Although these comments are anecdotal in nature, they are useful for understanding the concerns one may hear in a college or university, and have largely been addressed by the true definition of benchmarking as discussed earlier.

At a recent conference of the American Assembly of Collegiate Schools of Business (AACSB), a workshop was offered on benchmarking and Management Education Teaching and Curriculum (Bateman 1994). The discussion focused on how benchmarking was used for improving teaching and curriculum in the Graduate School of Business at the University of Chicago. For purposes of discussion, the following "straw objections" to the benchmarking were offered to the workshop participants:

- Euphemism for copying.
- Deterrent to innovation.
- Opportunity for plagiarism/industrial espionage.
- Promoter of inferior tactics since not invented here.
- Exposes organizational weaknesses.

Most of these concerns were addressed in previous sections on the definition of benchmarking and what it has to offer, such as W. Edwards Deming's comments on the hazards of copying without adapting. Other researchers, such as Dr. Howard Gitlow, have stated that an "example is no help in management unless studied with the aid of theory. To copy an example of success, without understanding it with the aid of theory, may lead to disaster" (Dale 1995, p. 12). Plagiarism and industrial espionage could indeed be disastrous, but they can be avoided if the benchmarking is done properly and the code of conduct is followed (see Appendix B). The lack of opportunity for innovation was also addressed in the previous discussion of benchmarking and its relationship to reengineering. Real innovation and breakthrough processes can be achieved, especially if an organization goes beyond benchmarking competitors, and does industry or generic benchmarking of world-class leaders, and adapts the processes back to the home industry. Benchmarking offers the ability to look externally at a very closed-minded organization or industry, which may believe that any processes, not invented within, are inferior. The practitioners of benchmarking state that it is difficult for faculty and college administrators to argue with data, and are therefore more compelled to make changes, than if the basis for change would be more subjective (Detrick et al. 1994; Detrick & Pica 1995). In addition, most benchmarking minimizes exposing organizational weaknesses, because the processes being examined are often not that confidential, and the benchmarking partner may be in a completely different industry.

Summary

Despite these concerns and criticisms, benchmarking is currently being used successfully in colleges and universities. As stated earlier, it is important to remember that benchmarking is more than just obtaining comparative numbers, it is part of a learning process within an organization. Bogan and English (1994) commented on the difference between benchmarking and benchmarks. They stated: *"benchmarks* (italics added) are measurements to gauge the performance of a function, operation, or business relative to others," whereas *benchmarking* is the "ongoing search for best practices that produce superior performance when adapted and implemented in one's organization" (Bogan and English 1994, p. 4). Since institutions of higher education profess learning, and value hard data, using benchmarking to improve our processes is a natural extension of what we provide to college students in the classroom.

BENCHMARKING IN HIGHER EDUCATION

The use of quality and continuous improvement techniques in higher education is in its fourth year, with campus efforts now numbering in the hundreds (Marchese 1995b). Several dozen of the more advanced programs involve benchmarking, conducted through consortia, professional associations, consulting companies, or individual efforts as it was originally done in the corporate world. Some of the projects to be examined are small and concentrate only on one area of academic or administrative processes. Other benchmarking efforts are larger and examine nearly every unit within the entire college or university. Each style, or method of conducting a benchmarking study, has benefits and drawbacks and should be chosen carefully by an institution considering benchmarking. First to be examined are the benchmarking studies sponsored by professional associations and consortia, such as the NACUBO project, graduate business schools, and continuing education (ACHE). Then, a wide selection of individual institution benchmarking efforts and interesting comments from some of the participants will be explored.

The NACUBO Project

Business officers are more aware than anyone else of the financial pressures that face higher education today due to spiraling costs and tuition, cutbacks in financial aid, the effects of a stagnant economy, decreasing state budgets, institutional operating budgets, and the costs of capital and quality improvement. In 1960, the National Federation of College and University Business Officers Association issued a report known as the Sixty College Study, which compared financial data for a nationwide sample of well-known liberal arts colleges (Bowen 1981). The results of this comparative study found wide differences in total educational and general expenditures per student for institutions of comparable size and mission. Before benchmarking was developed, most inter-institutional studies were firmly set on comparing only comparable organizations (not going outside of cohort groups), and they did not attempt to identify those institutions with best practices as true benchmarking does. A similar study was conducted by the Carnegie Commission on Higher Education in 1971, which assembled data on educational and general expenditures per FTE student for colleges and universities of various types.

Prior to the current benchmarking project, NACUBO conducted a study in the late 1980s in cooperation with the Council for the Advancement and Support of Education (CASE) which compared college fund-raising costs (McMillen 1990; Ryan 1990). This four-year study produced workable standards for capturing comparative costs useful to college administrators in fundraising, alumni administration, and public relations. Fifty-one institutions of higher education that completed the study reported their expenditures and gift income for the fiscal years 1985-1988. The study found that, on average, colleges spend about 16 cents to raise $1 in fundraising; however, the CASE report cautioned against simplistic reading of comparative study results, because the goal in fundraising activities is to maximize the net returns, not just to have the best percentage ratio. Although not labeled as such, it can be viewed as an early benchmarking effort and shows the value of comparative analysis in higher education.

The recent leading effort to address these problems with benchmarking was begun in late 1991 by the National Association of College and University Business Officers (AIR 1994; Kempner 1993; NACUBO 1995). Nearly 150 colleges and universities participated in the two-year pilot, which involved more than 1,600 individuals on 40 campuses. The project began by covering close to 40 functional areas with approximately 600 benchmarks, and it has been refined over the past four years based on participant feedback.

Currently, in the Fiscal Year 1995 NACUBO project, 26 core functions (14 fewer than when it started), plus two optional areas are offered in the benchmarking study. The goal of the NACUBO project is to encourage participating institutions to work together to discover best practices and provide institutions with the data they need for improvement of operations, that may cost too much or provide low quality service. The study is conducted by NACUBO, with the help of the Higher Education Consulting Group of the firm Coopers & Lybrand, and three other consulting firms. The cost of participation has decreased since the project first began in 1992 and varies depending on the scope and number of business functions. The current costs range from $5,000 to $14,000 and include new options that measure internal staff customer satisfaction. Typical processes within college and universities studied cover areas such as general accounting, alumni relations, accounts payable, admissions, accounts receivable, student registration, development, payroll, and purchasing. An example of the kind of data provided to participants is detailed in Table 4, which shows selected admissions benchmarks for different institutional types: public research, private research, public comprehensive, private comprehensive, and liberal arts.

TABLE 4

Selected Admission Benchmarks (Kempner 1993)

	A	B	C	D	E
Median applicants as a percentage of inquiries	20.3	11.4	29.2	12.6	19.4
Median offers as a percentage of applicants (first-year students)	74.3	80.8	76.6	75.3	77.0
Median acceptances as a percentage of offers (first-year students)	46.1	32.4	51.0	33.8	43.8
Average matriculants as a percentage of acceptances	94.9	97.1	94.6	96.3	97.6
Median high school and community college visits/admission FTE	14.8	11.5	28.6	27.9	31.4
Average calendar days required to process an application	21.5	24.1	15.3	21.7	17.0
A = public research B = private research C = public comprehensive D = private comprehensive E = liberal arts					

The NACUBO Benchmarking Project is different from earlier comparative studies because it does not seek to justify more dollars from state governments and donors, but seeks to use the results to cut costs and improve productivity (Massey & Myerson 1994). Traditionally, institutions have been primarily concerned with inputs and costs, where improved quality can only be achieved from greater expenditures. Benchmarking is different, because it focuses on the outputs and quality of services, not the inputs.

Different colleges and universities have decided to use

the data provided by the NACUBO project in different ways. Some participants, such as the State University of New York at Buffalo, used the benchmark data to improve the procurement practices in the purchasing office. Others, such as the Wheaton College in Massachusetts, used the benchmarking data to ensure that the TQM and Business Process Reengineering efforts address areas with the greatest potential for improvement (Kempner 1993). The NACUBO data offers the opportunity to introduce the concept of reengineering for those processes that need to be completely redesigned. This high-profile project has greatly increased the awareness of benchmarking within the field of higher education, and it offers insight into the correlation between the financial cost inputs of resources and the outputs of operational services.

All 20 campuses and the system offices of the California State University participated in the 1993 NACUBO project (Sundstrom 1995). They limited their participation to cover the accounts payable, admissions, central budgeting, facilities, financial aid, general accounting, treasury and cash management, human resources, payroll, procurement, registration and records, student accounts receivable, and billing. There were a total of 172 institutions in the 1993 project, and Cal State made both extramural comparisons with representative cohorts and internal comparisons with other system campuses. When asked what quantifiable quality or efficiency improvements resulted from the NACUBO participation, David Sundstrom, University Auditor, stated:

In a word, there were many positive results from benchmarking. Sixteen of our universities are participating in the 1995 project. We think that we learned a lot from our first year's efforts and know that this year's data will be more accurate and valuable. We also look forward to longitudinal studies to get a better understanding of the positive effects of the many process reengineering projects that are underway (p. 2).

However, not everyone agrees that the NACUBO project is useful, or appropriate, as it is conducted. Some participants believe that there is too high a level of data aggregation, and that the results are too detailed to be really useful (Bateman 1994). Once the participants receive the rather large benchmarking report from NACUBO, the results may often be passed around from one office to another with little accountability for implementation. Others believe that what is missing from the NACUBO study is the participation of the customer, or user of the data, from each of the institutional units. In addition, the lack of information on academic departments, and the unavailability of cohort information for nonparticipants has also been criticized (Gaither et al. 1994). Bruce Stark from Colorado State University added that he sees no correlation between what NACUBO did and true benchmarking, as defined in Robert Camp's 1989 bench-marking book, because they did not follow the original 10-step process outlined (Stark 1995). In addition, the NACUBO does not appear to find the "best of the best" by looking outside the field of higher education, as Xerox did when it looked at the operations of L. L. Bean. Stark sug-gested that colleges and universities might start by looking at internal training programs, such as Motorola University, where they often do a better job of assessing the training and education needs of their people than higher education does. Some of these criticisms have been heard by NACUBO, and the ongoing benchmarking project is still evolving with each yearly iteration.

GMAC/EBI Benchmarking Project

Business schools often teach about TQM, BPR, and bench-marking topics in their undergraduate and graduate courses and programs. Recently, these techniques have also been used to improve the quality of the delivery and administra-tion of graduate business programs. When members of the American Assembly of Collegiate Schools of Business (AACSB), the main accrediting body for business schools, and the Graduate Management Admission Council (GMAC) began to consider benchmarking activities of their members, two individuals stepped forward to conduct a pilot study (AACSB 1994): Joe Pica, assistant dean and MBA program director at Indiana University, and Glenn Detrick, an educa-tional consultant and former vice president of educational programs with the GMAC. They worked with business schools in the Big Ten Conference to conduct a pilot bench-marking study in the 1993-94 academic year. Participants from the schools met to discuss common problems they faced and to consider solutions using benchmarking. Pica stated, "I've always believed in fact-based decision-making

. . . when we first discussed the pilot study, we found that our colleagues were very motivated to obtain hard data, but their desire for information was beyond their ability to collect it" (AACSB 1994, p. 16). The pilot study showed that a group of competing schools could be forthright about their own institutional processes and could share potentially sensitive information. The study established a basic language and standards for data reporting, because common definitions of simple terms for graduate admission processes did not exist before. In addition, it was reported that just participating in the study provided a useful means of measuring internal operational effectiveness, even before competition data was received. This comment is echoed by participants in other benchmarking studies, including the ACHE project discussed next. One real value of benchmarking is this introspection, which forces participants to go inside their own institution, collect information, and raise questions (Detrick & Pica 1995). During the first year of the pilot study, benchmark data gathered from business schools included processes such as those in Table 5.

Other benchmarks were also gathered on demographic and biographic application information. Representatives in the pilot study found that participating was a positive experience, and has been helpful in self-analysis, in preparing budget requests, and in getting additional resources. For

TABLE 5

Sample GMAC/EBI Benchmark Processes (Detrick et al. 1994)

Process Measured	Results Range (approximate)
Applications received per recruiting FTE staff	170-290
Admits per recruiting-admissions FTE staff	40-160
Cost per viewbook	$1.00-$5.00
Percentage of applicants admitted	25-80% (domestic)
Percent of admits that matriculate	40-60% (domestic)

example, Don Bell, MBA program director at the University of Minnesota, found that he was able to identify two significant internal problems that had not previously come to his attention, and was then able to take action based on the data obtained and make immediate improvements. Ken Bardach, MBA program director at Michigan State University added that "benchmarking forces us to do the things that good managers want to do but find excuses not to . . . It forces us to put mirrors around us, look at what we're doing, and see if we re doing it well" (AACSB 1994, p. 17). Overall, the participating business schools see benchmarking as a critical catalyst for change, and it reduces, or eliminates, resistance to improvement because resistors find it difficult to dispute hard data.

The success of the pilot study led Pica and Detrick to form a consulting company called Educational Benchmarking, Inc. (EBI) and then offer to conduct a full study. In the Fall of 1994, 68 schools paid $1,500 to participate in the first year of the study. A 20-page summary of the results was delivered the following year, and 600 hundred invitations were then sent for participation in the second year of the study (Pica 1995). EBI plans to add a student satisfaction benchmarking survey in 1996, and it is also considering benchmarking faculty productivity in the future. The kind of benchmarking that EBI and the business schools are doing has been highly effective, because it is developed and used by the personnel involved in the actual implementation of the processes studied. Other benchmarking projects are often initiated at a very senior level within a college or university, and the results never reach, and/or do not have the ownership of the units responsible, in order to make effective improvements.

Overall, the participating business schools see benchmarking as a critical catalyst for change, and it reduces, or eliminates, resistance to improvement because resistors find it difficult to dispute hard data.

ACHE Competitive Benchmarking Study

In 1995, the Association for Continuing Higher Education (ACHE) funded a benchmarking project, conducted by the author of this report, to measure the administrative processes and financial ratios associated with noncredit course and program management (Alstete 1996). A cover letter and a 33-item questionnaire were mailed to the 300 institutional members of the ACHE in August 1995. A follow-up letter and second questionnaire were sent one month later to all non-respondents. A total of 82 surveys (27 percent) were returned, 57 (19 percent) of which were usable for the project. Many of the 33 questions in the survey required the sometimes laborious computation of ratios and percentages of current administrative activities, and financial ratios for non-credit programs. Several respondents commented to the researcher that the mere activity of calculating these ratios and percentages for the survey was of use to them in analyzing their administration. The results are intended to provide an external perspective on administrative practices, identify best practices, and specify areas for improvement in the reader's noncredit program management.

Since many, if not most, noncredit programs offered by offices of continuing education are required to be self-sustaining financially, a key benchmark identified by the participants was the financial surplus ratio. This kind of ratio may not be a key indicator for other departments in colleges or universities, but it is merely being shown as an example of how certain benchmark information was presented to search for best practices in noncredit continuing education. This key benchmark measured the percent surplus generated by dividing the remaining dollars (after all administrative and instructional costs) by the total revenue generated for non-credit courses. The average financial surplus generated for all participants was found to be 20.6 percent, and a median of 15 percent. The top 12 performing institutions on this particular benchmark were identified as the "leaders," because they had a financial surplus of 30 percent or greater. As a point of reference, a comparison with the process leaders is used throughout the analysis reported to the participants. However, the most important comparison will be with the participants own institutional benchmarks for process improvement efforts. The differences between the full group of participants and the financial surplus leaders appear in the sample process benchmark questions shown in Table 6.

Inquiry response time measured the average number of days to mail out a catalog/brochure to prospective students who inquire. The average response time for all participants was 8.4 days, with a median of 2 days. The leaders had an average of 2.6 days and a median of 1.6 days. The inquiry-to-registration conversion ratio showed that, on average, the leaders outperformed the entire group of participants in the study by converting more inquiries into registered students. The annual registrations to administrative staff ratio found that the financial surplus leaders have a lower ratio of staff

TABLE 6

**Sample ACHE Competitive Benchmarking Study Results
(Alstete 1996, p.28)**

All Participants	Inquiry Response	Registration Converts (%)	Ann. Regist. /Staff Ratio	New Courses Offered (%)
Average	8.4	39.2	1196.2	22.4
Median	2	40	900	15
Maximum	90	85	7000	95
Minimum	1	1	10	2
Leaders				
Average	2.6	59.9	558.8	23.5
Median	1.58	75	359	20
Maximum	8	85	2000	51
Minimum	1	8	10	5

to students. The percentage of new courses offered had a higher median (20 percent) for the financial leaders than for all study participants (15 percent). This may suggest that the more financially successful programs try out more new courses. Although this data is interesting to see how different institutions perform, the real benefits are in how it can be used by participating continuing education administrators. Information on the processes of all participants can be compared with leaders, analyzed for effectiveness, and decisions can be made if improvement efforts are warranted at the home institution. If a participating institution discovers an area of a noncredit program that is not efficient or overly expensive compared to peers, it now has data to attempt improvement efforts. One part missing from this benchmarking project is the ability to identify and visit competitive institutions, as some consortium and most individual benchmarking studies offer the participants.

Consortium Studies
Other methods of obtaining benchmarking data include

consortium studies organized by institutions interested in freely sharing information. One of earliest such studies was the Study of Independent Higher Education in Indiana conducted in the mid-1970s (Jellema & Oliver 1975). This project was underwritten by the Lily Endowment, and it was commissioned by the Associated Colleges of Indiana and the Independent Colleges and Universities of Indiana, Inc., whose joint boards acted as a steering committee for the study. In its year of operation, the study produced six reports on institutional goals, the cost of instruction, student characteristics and finances, financial health, inter-institutional cooperation, and economic impact. Twenty-nine of the 32 independent, four-year accredited institutions in the State of Indiana participated in this early example of a competitive benchmarking-type study. The findings were used for comparative purposes to provide each institution with a historical benchmark for planning and making projections. Many of these goals overlap with the objectives of benchmarking, as we define it today.

A more recent consortium-sponsored project is currently being conducted by the University of Delaware National Study of Institutional Costs and Productivity, and it is funded for three years by the Fund for Improvement of Postsecondary Education. The study will survey 160 institutions, of which 35 are research, 45 doctoral-granting, and 75 are comprehensive colleges and universities (Middaugh 1995). Additional data sharing consortia include the Higher Education Data Sharing Consortium and the Public University Data Sharing Consortium (which is no longer active), the Southern University Data Sharing Consortium (Middaugh & Hollowell 1992), and the National Cooperative Data Share - Benchmark Data Exchange by John Minter Associates (Minter 1996). Data sharing consortia such as these can make uniform and consistent inter-institutional comparison feasible and cost-effective. They routinely conduct studies to collect data on academic and administrative workloads, staffing and funding patterns, and other variables across the spectrum of participating institutions. These consortia are often organized by administrators from offices of institutional research, and they routinely organize special interest meetings at the annual Association for Institutional Researchers Forum.

The National Cooperative Data Share - Benchmark Data

Exchange is a subscription service currently available on the World Wide Web at http://www.edmin.com/jma/ncds.html. Its purpose is to provide timely, relevant, and accessible comparative information for planning and budgeting, but could possibly be used as a beginning for a true benchmarking search for best practices. An institution wishing to examine its revenue contribution ratios, expenditure allocation ratios, faculty salary files, enrollments, retention, and other data can pull the appropriate data from hundreds of institutions across the nation (Minter 1996).

One discipline-specific professional association that sponsors data sharing and offers advice for process improvement is the Learning Resources Network through their publication titled "Ratios for Success" (LERN 1992). This international association provides information on class programming and consulting expertise to organizations offering classes for adults, including colleges and universities, public schools, hospitals and community groups. The LERN association states that this publication provides ratios that are intended to be "pegs" or "guideposts," that can be used by program administrators to reduce guesswork when planning educational programs. Forty-two ratios are listed and cover general costs, promotion costs, financial ratios, and course enrollment calculations. The following example for the New Course Cancellation Rates show how the ratios are listed for the LERN association members who purchase the report.

Ratio: New Course Cancellation Rates
- Definition: A "new" course is one which has not been offered before.
- Ideal: 30-50 percent of new courses
- Importance: Understanding the course cancellation rates for new courses versus the old successful courses will help you improve your product mix.
- Explanation: New courses ought to have a higher cancellation rate than old courses. New courses have not yet been offered; you are experimenting, trying new ideas. Thus, if your Old Course Cancellation Rate is in the tolerable range, you can tolerate a much higher cancellation rate for your new courses . . . .
- Related Ratios: See also "Number of New Courses to Offer;" "Number of Old Courses to Offer;" and "Old Course Cancellation Rate" (LERN 1992, p. 41).

The LERN organization states that the ratios provided are based on 15 years of research into educational programming. However, true benchmarking does more than just provide recommended ratios, it should also uncover the most successful organizations that have the best practices and discover how they achieve the successful results. The ratios provided by LERN, although not based entirely on comparative data, may still be useful in non-credit program planning. The information would be of much greater value if the recommended ratios were more specific, identified the performance leaders, and their means of achieving success. In addition, real benchmarking involves more than just sharing data in one industry; it should also include seeking out truly outstanding processes that may be outside higher education, and adapting these best practices to the home institution. This is what many of the individual, institutional benchmarking projects that will now be reviewed are doing currently.

Individual Benchmarking Projects

The nonprofit status and decentralized nature of higher education makes it easy to see why many colleges and universities adapted the aforementioned benchmarking consortia arrangements, through professional associations or hiring independent consulting companies. However, on their own, many colleges have also done internal, competitive, industry, and even generic benchmarking as it was originally defined in business and industry. In the recent past, colleges and universities have on occasion conducted studies and research that compare processes, but they leave out the important benchmarking goal of adapting best practices. The goal of these comparative studies is often to measure cost-effectiveness or simply to decide which institution is best, based on numbers. One example of an internal benchmarking-like study was conducted at the University of Delaware, where internal academic and administrative productive ratios and cost containment strategies were calculated and compared (Middaugh & Hollowell 1992). Staffing and productivity ratios were analyzed across departments and used for budgetary planning decisions. The authors reporting on this project comment on the potential usefulness of inter-institutional data (competitive benchmarking) to compare academic and administrative workloads. Another example of a pre-benchmarking comparative study was conducted in the early-1980s by the State University of New York (SUNY) at Fredonia (Reimann 1995). The study involved comparing the effectiveness on student achievement of their General College Program (GCP) curriculum with Miami University of Ohio, which had no such program. Test achievements from sample student groups from each institution were paired, and the results showed a greater maturation rate for Fredonia's students compared to Miami's. Again, this is similar to competitive benchmarking and shows that there are precedents in which institutions of higher education have freely shared data and compared practices. Even articles published this year continue to use the term benchmarking when it is marginally appropriate. A study titled "Benchmarking Academic Credit and Noncredit Continuing Education" (Brewer, Hale, and McLaurin 1996) is a descriptive survey of organizational structures and administrative practices within the University System of Georgia. According to the authors, the purpose of this information is to prepare for the next step of benchmarking that will determine the reasons behind the differences uncovered in the first study.

An example of benchmarking that is closer to the true definition of the process was conducted at Oregon State University in the early 1990s as part of its overall effort to reshape the university with restructuring and process-reengineering (Coate 1992). The consultants that OSU hired recommended that they should use a peer group list rather than an "aspirant group" list of institutions that represent their current cohorts, and not models for significant improvement. Their goal was to discover problem areas and build up the reasoning for radical change. OSU developed a list of eight universities to benchmark: Colorado State, Cornell, Iowa State, Kansas State, North Carolina State, Oklahoma State, Oregon, and Washington State. At one point, the committee conducting the project decided to include at least one "aspirant" university (Cornell), as well as the other peer group institutions. The consultants suggested that the peer institutions could provide the much needed general data to match with OSU and universities, such as Cornell, that were "best in class." These would be used for benchmarking some individual processes. The benchmarking methodology proceeded at OSU when the university president sent a cover letter, along with the benchmark survey form, to the president of each university in the project. In addition, a tele-

have been using benchmarking initiatives in a wide variety of areas within the University. Louise Sandmeyer (1995) commented:

> *This year all budget executives were asked to include in their strategic plans a plan for benchmarking. Administrators were asked to include in their plans a determination of what criteria to use in establishing benchmark quality indicators, benchmark processes, and benchmark universities, colleges, and departments. Initially, units have been asked to collect internal data and initiate collection of data from comparable units, compare and analyze internal and external data, and discuss implications for strategic goals and action plans. It is expected that over time, units will examine processes that enable other units to achieve superior performance, and units are being encouraged to understand the processes and practices that make a program or department best in class . . . Our TQM Forum partner, Dupont, delivered a benchmarking course on campus and have shared their benchmarking materials with us . . . The process improvement model [that] we are encouraging CQI teams to follow includes a benchmarking step, and many of our teams have benchmarked their processes . . . As part of CQI training, a 3 hour introduction to benchmarking course is regularly offered through the Human Resource Development Center. When reviewing the benchmarking section of the strategic plans, we found that there is considerable comparative analysis going on. Some units have begun to identify core processes and are establishing benchmarking assessment teams. We continue to profit from our corporate partners who keep us on track and emphasize the importance of benchmarking processes for improvement, and not just the collection of data to prove how good we are* (p. 4).

Other colleges, such as Babson College, have focused their individual institutional benchmarking efforts primarily on the business transactions processes. Gerry Shaw (1995) from Babson summarized their efforts, which, like Pennsylvania State University above, involve real generic benchmarking and searches for best practices outside of higher education:

One of the processes involved here is the registration process. Recognizing that this process has a number of sub-processes, benchmarking in this area has taken on diverse areas. So far, we have met with representatives from hotels (around the registration and check-in process), Disney (around the technology and "smart card"), banks, and a few other organizations (around the billing process), Chrylser Corp. (around the customer focus area), a Big Six accounting firm (around the technology they use for the recruiting process), and other institutions of higher education (who have already begun to do what we are aiming to do). We have not gained much from the NACUBO study. The benchmarking work (we have done) has helped us a great deal. We have learned where and what to avoid as we move along, how others have dealt with resistance along the way, how technology can be used to better enable what we are trying to do, and how to achieve a stronger customer focus. We have found the various companies we have contacted to be very interested in what we are doing and very open and willing to help us (p. 4-5).

Benchmarking does not have to be complex or very highly structured in order to be effective. One simple project was conducted at the University of Chicago's Graduate School of Business (Bateman 1994). An internal benchmarking project involving management education was done by the MBA students in an effort to improve teaching. The students ranked each faculty member's teaching and described why there were differences. Speaking at a recent AACSB Continuous Improvement Conference, George Bateman from the School of Business stated that the results were surprisingly well-received. He believes that administrative and academic quality efforts are inextricably linked, and stated that if a college or university is applying quality only to the administration side, they are missing a lot. Academic and administration need to be linked in quality improvement efforts.

Geno Schnell from the Office of Continuous Quality Improvement at the University of Maryland, reported that benchmarking has been used successfully to reduce the processing time for surplus property requests:

Benchmarking does not have to be complex or very highly structured in order to be effective.

*When the need for a new surplus property process
arose, the Department of Procurement and Supply created a CQI action to study how campus departments
could be served better. Up to that point, departments
with excess equipment or furniture were required to
keep the property in their departments, until a new
owner could be identified within, or outside, the
University. On average, it took more than 74 days to
process a surplus property request. The team seized
upon the construction of a new central distribution
facility on campus and designed a surplus operation
. . . Now, when departments determine that they have
unneeded property, they can schedule an immediate
pick up. As soon as it arrives . . . it is available for purchase rather than awaiting an annual surplus property
auction. The team designed this operation using continuous feedback from campus customers and benchmarking to 18 other surplus property operations in the
U.S. and Canada* (1995, p. 6).

Benchmarking in higher education is also being conducted at several European institutions. For example, the graduate business school benchmarking efforts discussed earlier
have been applied to European management schools
(Detrick et al. 1994; Detrick & Pica 1995). Also, Art Clarke
from Sir Sanford Fleming College stated that benchmarking
is being used as part of an overall quality improvement and
competitive analysis program at his institution:

*The notion of benchmarks, while not new, has not been
considered in earnest until recently. Growth was
encouraged and funded. In this heady, expansive
atmosphere the established standards were broad and
general, making them easy to achieve. Additionally,
while the colleges are bounded by a variety of legislated
requirements, within these, each college is fiercely
autonomous. How times have changed! Many factors
have joined to decrease the rate of increase in the funding that the colleges receive from the province. In fact
this year, the colleges had to return 3% of their grants.
"Competitiveness," in the sense that the private sector
uses it, is now part of how the public sector must operate. Thus [there is] the interest in partnerships and joint*

*ventures, program rationalization, TQM, CQI, stand-
ards, and benchmarks. Our ministry publishes data
comparing the colleges on a variety of expenditures: full
and part-time faculty, administrative costs, professional
development expenditures, and so forth. An analysis of
faculty workloads across the system has been completed.
While benchmarks are implied in this data, the effort to
establish them has just begun. Fleming has only begun
the process of arriving at benchmarks. The Board of
Governs and the Senior Management Team have done
some work to identify performance indicators.
Benchmarks will be developed from these. We are
uncertain whether to use internal criteria or external
criteria such as other colleges, government departments,
or private sectors organizations* (1995, p. 5).

Other overseas benchmarking studies include a project in
the Department of Counseling and Health at Queensland
University of Technology, Australia (Jackson 1995). They
are working with a benchmarking team from the international student services section and Careers and Employment
Services office. The goal is to benchmark processes used
for translating client input into service requirements and use
these requirements for services planning and implementation. This will be accomplished using quantitative questionnaires and qualitative research from focus groups. Although
the first stage is a noncompetitive internal benchmarking
project, it will lead to comparative external benchmarking
activities, as well.

Harvard Business School has also used benchmarking to
improve the delivery of their prominent graduate business
programs. Faculty members actively visited nearly two
dozen traditional business schools in the United States and
abroad, as well as corporate training programs, and other
selected institutions to collect information. Harvard wanted
to compare itself to its competitors, and use the data to provide a better MBA program. The "External Comparisons
Project Team" was influenced by the extent of dramatic
change that is occurring in business schools they visited, and
concluded that MBA programs are redefining the nature of
management education (HBS 1993). The report that resulted
from this project uses text and figures to compare the curriculum of traditional MBA programs with the new designs

they found. The Harvard case is an example of benchmarking done by and for faculty in higher education.

In some colleges and universities, benchmarking and quality concepts have been accepted and used by both faculty and administration to help convert the institutions into true learning organizations. Several institutions of higher education have used the concepts and criteria of the Malcolm Baldrige National Quality Award (MBNQA) in their planning processes and outcomes measurements (Seymour 1996). Continuous quality improvement and the use of real benchmarking techniques to search for best practices are an integral part of the Baldrige Criteria, along with an overall goal of continuous organizational learning. As stated earlier in this report, the MBNQA criteria was adapted for education (see Appendix A), and a full MBNQA Pilot Study was conducted in 1995 at Northwest Missouri State University. A "Culture of Quality," originated at Northwest Missouri State in the mid-1980s, incorporates a systematic search for best practice ideas to enhance administrative efficiency in the University. This process started in the administrative areas and grew to improving undergraduate education, and the overall quality of the university. After implementing many best practice ideas and benefiting greatly from these benchmarking and quality improvement efforts, the planners at Northwest Missouri State University concluded that a simple repeat of their search for best practices would not be as beneficial as it was the first time. They considered several options and decided to use the MBNQA as a template for continuous quality improvement.

The education-adapted MBNQA criteria, as implemented at Northwest Missouri State University, uses external comparisons, benchmarking, and the search for best practices throughout the seven categories used for scoring: leadership, information and analysis, strategic and operation planning, human resource development and management, educational and business process management, institutional performance results, student focus and student and stakeholder satisfaction (Seymour 1996). For example, in the leadership category 1.1 (senior administrative leadership, worth 40 points), real benchmarking can be seen:

> *Against the background of a focused mission and chal-*
> *lenging megatrends, faculty, staff, and students were*

*asked to identify "best practices" through a benchmark-
ing process. As part of the process, faculty teams
reviewed all available recent literature, along with the
so-called "reform literature" relating to undergraduate
education. Additionally, the nation's best known leaders in higher education were contacted for their best
practice ideas. At the end of the process, over 200 best
practice ideas were identified and cataloged* (Seymour
1996, vol. 2, p. 36).

Northwest Missouri State University did more than just
use external data comparisons, as many other institutions do
when conducting "benchmarking." They searched for best
practices and implemented the findings across the University
in many different departments and areas of measurement,
including strategic and operational planning (category 3). In
addition, benchmarking is actually the primary focus in the
second category 2.2 - Comparisons and Benchmarking. The
description of this category details how comparisons and
benchmarking data are selected and used to help drive
improvement of overall performance, how needs and priorities are determined, criteria for seeking appropriate information and data, how the information and data are used to set
improvement targets, and/or encourage breakthrough
approaches, and finally how Northwest evaluates and
improves its overall benchmarking process (Seymour 1996).
Of all the individual institutions using benchmarking,
Northwest Missouri State University's pursuit of the MBNQA
is perhaps the most thorough application of benchmarking
in higher education uncovered for this report.

Benefits and Concerns for Higher Education
In most of the cases where benchmarking was conducted,
positive comments were made about benchmarking activities at colleges and universities, and that external pressures
for the use of benchmarking could help speed implementation. Ray Carlson, from Dalhousie University, believes that
benchmarking is a much needed comparative analysis technique, and he described the future plans for benchmarking
at his institution:

*From my perspective, benchmarking is probably the key
to CQI being useful on campus. At the same time,*

benchmarking relies on some form of outcome meas-
urement—as one can measure outcomes in a valid and
reliable way, it becomes possible to identify processes
that seem more effective, and then try to isolate factors
that might be responsible, and test whether introduction
of these factors leads to better results. In this perspec-
tive, readiness for benchmarking is basically an issue of
readiness to directly assess outcome. In the long-run,
we hope to include all facets of our operations, but at
the moment, this means the best results relate to those
facets that have easily assessable results: e.g., registra-
tion activities assessed in relation to time required and
number of unsuccessful requests, time required in pur-
chasing books, success in getting access to a computer,
use of CD-ROMs, application for research funding to
different sources, annual fund campaigns, [and] attend-
ance at various events. It is important, though, to move
this to the academic and knowledge-production facets
of our operations. Currently, we can use our existing
course evaluation procedures to look at best practices in
terms of generating student satisfaction, as long as we
isolate comparable academic activities, e.g., courses
that are similar in size, pressure to enroll, and general
content. We have tentatively decided to experiment
with assessment devices, that might allow comparisons,
in terms of student learning, for certain types of courses
and knowledge pay-off for certain types of research, but
such activities are still in the discussion stage. We are
likely to move faster when there is external pressure for
such benchmarking (1995, p. 7).

However, external pressures can also work against a college or university. When the benchmarking process is initi-
ated by departments, such as a school of business or a
purchasing office, it is clear what the goals of the project are
and what benefits can be expected by the participants. It
was also stated earlier that benchmarking is often used inap-
propriately or misdefined and can sometimes be used for
purposes other than finding best practices. Dave Sill, from
Southern Illinois University, related how the term benchmarking was used by the Illinois Board of Higher Education
for purposes other than its definition originally intended
(1995). The State of Illinois Board of Higher Education

developed a benchmarking process which they titled Priority-Quality-Productivity (P-Q-P), beginning in 1992. Twenty-five guidelines were to be considered in making productivity improvements in five areas: instruction, research and public service, overall academic functions, administrative functions, and state policies affecting higher education. However, the P-Q-P process as it relates to benchmarking does not contain a systematic search for best practices as real benchmarking does. Those individuals at the state level, in charge of setting the benchmarks, are external and removed from the units in the colleges and universities being benchmarked. Sill (1995) stated that ". . . because of a lack of familiarity with operations in the affected units, they have set benchmarks that are arbitrary and in some cases highly distorted. There is no local ownership of the process" (1995, p. 8).

The literature reviewed often states that local ownership is critical for success of a quality improvement process such as benchmarking, but many colleges and universities have continued to receive external prodding for process improvement, and some have had successful results. Another example of state-mandated quality improvements that involved benchmarking was at Oregon State University in the early 1990s (Coate 1992; Coate 1993). OSU began implementing total quality management in late 1989 in response to state-mandated administrative cost/structure assessment, that sought to increase effectiveness, efficiency, and reduce costs. Benchmarking was one of the many TQM tools used, which included organizational restructuring, process reengineering, outsourcing and elimination, and elimination of unnecessary bureaucracy. The president's TQM team at OSU started the benchmarking component by asking 67 alumni, students, faculty members, business people and others, what areas needed improvement. The issues or processes of top importance were found to be: admission, recruiting/marketing, administrative communication, and to a lesser extent, the development office (Coate 1993). The team decided that their benchmarking effort should have the primary goal of improving the recruiting/marketing process of the university and improve the responsiveness of the admission process. OSU's president then established five separate TQM teams to study the following major customer problems:

1. Admissions paperwork and telephone processes.
2. Graduate admissions process, with the Graduate School Office.
3. Admissions evaluation criteria and process.
4. Recruiting and marketing, with admission and University Relations.
5. Admission post-acceptance process, with the Alumni Office.

As part of the project, the TQM team analyzed the paperwork and telephone process by examining 100 admission files at random. They were disappointed at the average length of turnaround time they found for processing documents, especially compared to that found at the University of Oregon, a comparable institution. The team then conducted a data collection tour at the University of Oregon, gathering information on people, equipment, and processes that deal with reception and phones, incoming and outgoing mail, coding and processing of applications, and evaluation of applications. The "best practices," as correctly defined by benchmarking, were discovered to be the assembly line system that could be adapted back to OSU and solve their timeliness problem. The team leader reported, "Benchmarking saved us a year of time . . . [The University of] Oregon was a year ahead of us implementing a new software system . . . Our paper flow was still patterned after the old system, and it wasn't working" (Coate 1993, p. 29). In order to monitor improvements, the team plans to pull 100 files periodically and chart the turnaround time for processing. Other processes were also improved in this benchmarking project, such as the phone answering. These state-mandated quality improvement and cost reduction requirements actually created some fans of TQM and benchmarking at OSU. However, most practitioners would agree that, if there is local ownership of the process improvement techniques, then there is a much higher likelihood for successful implementation and adaption of best practices.

STARTING A BENCHMARKING PROCESS

We have seen how benchmarking was developed in the business world and how it is used today in a variety of colleges and universities. But where does a reader interested in setting up the process improvement technique called "benchmarking" begin? Many of the books and articles on the topic have the starting process well-defined. Although benchmarking is not difficult, a great amount of thought, internal study, and research must be conducted before embarking on a benchmarking effort (Brigham 1995). In Belmont University's Quality Team Manual on Benchmarking (1993), seven points are listed for consideration before beginning to benchmark and are paraphrased as follows:

1. Is there already a focus in your work area or department around service, employees, and continuous improvement of processes?
2. Is benchmarking the right strategy in this situation? (According to the International Quality Study, world-class benchmarking is only suitable for already high-performing organizations. Competitive or peer benchmarking is more appropriate for low or medium performing organizations.)
3. What should you benchmark? Choose those processes that align with the organizational mission and contribute to the organization's long-term success.
4. What should you measure? You are attempting to generate comparative performance data; you are observing how they achieved those results.
5. What organization(s) should you benchmark? The ideal one would have a higher performance level than you do in the specific area being benchmarked.
6. How should you collect data? First, establish internal baseline performance measures. Then be creative for tracking down other sources of data.
7. How can you implement what you learned? Determine the variances between your processes and those benchmarked. Separate out, if necessary, unique factors either to the benchmarked organization or to higher education. Then, develop a mission statement for the process, and set clear goals and action plans.

Belmont University's seven points are sound, and they reflect the original definition and intent of benchmarking.

Benchmarking efforts that are undertaken too quickly, or conducted in a top-down approach from the senior administration level, with little or no input from mid-level users of the data, often do not realize how important it is to properly plan what to benchmark, against whom, how to collect the data, and how to analyze and use the results. However, one important element missing is the selection of who in the college or university will actually conduct the benchmarking project. Most of the literature reviewed recommends the creation of a benchmarking team, especially if the benchmarking project is not to be primarily conducted by a professional association or data-sharing consortium.

Spendolini (1992) stated that there are indeed some explicit qualifications for benchmarking team members that should be considered before beginning the project. Some colleges and universities may be restricted by size in the choices they can make, but it is still wise to consider these attributes, and therefore, maximize the effectiveness of the team (or committee) choices that are available. The first specific characteristic recommended is functional expertise and a demonstrated level of job skills, or work-related performance, in the position they hold at the institution. Second, the employee should have sufficient credibility in the institution, as judged by subject-matter knowledge, employment history, and the level of position(s) held. Benchmarking team members should also have above average communication skills, in order to communicate well with other team members and the benchmark project partners at other organizations. Lastly, Spendolini recommended that effective benchmarkers need to have a high level of team spirit, including a sense of cooperation, effective listening skills, an ability to reach a consensus, and respect for the opinions of others. Dale (1995) added that the "perfect" team member will be implementing changes, is hands-on, action oriented, has nothing else to do, is a super salesperson, and is creative and flexible. The optimal team size, according to Dale, is five members, who are from multiple disciplines and personalities. Once the team is selected, the next step should be the selection of the topic(s) for the benchmarking study.

Deciding What to Benchmark
Process benchmarking studies analyze the processes or prac-

tices that are important to the performance of the organization (APQC 1993). The catalyst for the study may be identified from institutional problem areas uncovered, internal or external strategic change initiatives, or the currently popular continuous quality improvement efforts. A basic lesson learned in the quality movement relates to processes and the Pareto Principle, which states that 20 percent of all activity affects 80 percent of the results (Watson, 1993). Therefore, the focus of improvement efforts should be on those few critical processes that have the highest potential for "return on attention," as Watson labeled it. *Processes* are often chosen to be benchmarked because they have a broader range than *business practices*, and are important for achieving *critical success factors* (APQC 1993). The American Productivity and Quality Center defines these terms for business and other organizations, and the definitions have been expanded to include examples of their use in higher education:

. . . the focus of improvement efforts should be on those few critical processes that have the highest potential for "return on attention" . . .

- *Business processes* are logical combinations of people, equipment, materials, and methods that [are] organized into work activities to produce a given output. These activities have varying levels of scope. The underlying principles of TQM include the concept that organizations basically consist of a set of interrelated processes, nested within each other. For colleges and universities, these processes include the broad administration of the college, within the supervision process of academic departments, and which include the actual process of course instruction.
- *Critical success factors* (CSFs) are those characteristics, conditions, or variables that have a direct influence on a customer's satisfaction with specific business process[es] and therefore, on the success of the entire process. Examples of CSFs for higher education include regional and professional accreditations, student evaluations, competitive rankings, graduation and placement rates, service levels, etc.
- *Business practices* are methods, or approaches, that facilitate the execution of a process. For example, the self-study for accreditation is a process for colleges and universities. The business practice is to base the criteria for self-study on the regional accrediting body or professional association's criteria for self-assessment (adapted from APQC 1993, pp.6-7).

In order to help guide benchmarking teams, to link the processes to be analyzed, with important critical success factors, Spendolini (1992) stated that Xerox asks employees to consider the following 10 questions:

1. *What is the most critical factor to my function/organization's success (e.g., customer satisfaction, expense to revenue ratio, return on asset performance)?*
2. *What factors are causing the most trouble (e.g., not performing to expectations)?*
3. *What products or services are provided to customers?*
4. *What factors account for customer satisfaction?*
5. *What specific problems (operational) have been identified in the organization?*
6. *Where are the competitive pressures being felt in the organization?*
7. *What are the major costs (or cost "drivers") in the organization?*
8. *Which functions represent the highest percentage of cost?*
9. *Which functions have the greatest room for improvement?*
10. *Which functions have the greatest effect (or potential) for differentiating the organization from competitors in the marketplace?* (p. 71)

These questions help the benchmarking participants prioritize the potential benchmarking processes based on need. The main focus of these questions are on cost reduction, problem reduction, customer satisfaction, continuous improvement, and marketplace superiority, each of which could accurately be defined as a critical success factor. Additional advice includes the benchmarking SMART acronym, which means that the processes are Specific, Measurable, Achievable, Realistic, and Timeframed (Dale 1995).

If an organization is conducting benchmarking because a problem has already been uncovered, on a process or business practice (problem-based benchmarking), then the identification of what to benchmark should not be difficult. If, however, an institution is not immediately sure where to begin, then deciding what processes to benchmark must be planned thoroughly (process-based benchmarking). Participants in organized benchmarking studies, such as NACUBO, can choose from more than 26 institutional areas and processes to analyze, or benchmark them all (see Table 8).

TABLE 8

Functional Areas in the NACUBO National Benchmarking Survey (NACUBO 1995, p. 39).

Core Functional Areas

1. Academic Affairs	16. Info. Technology/ Telecomm.*
2. Accounts Payable*	17. Payroll
3. Admissions	18. Purchasing
4. Alumni Relations	19. Registration and Records*
5. Bookstore*	20. Risk Management*
6. Central Budget Department	21. Sponsored Projects*
7. Collections*	22. Student Accounts Receivable*
8. Development Office	23. Student Health Services
9. Facilities*	24. Student Housing
10. Financial Aid*	25. Treasury-Cash Management
11. Food Services	26. Overall Indicators and Ratios
12. General Accounting*	
13. Human Resources— General	Optional Sections
14. Human Resources— Benefits Administration	1. Multi-Campus System Administration
15. Human Resources—Hiring	2. Data for Institutions with Hospitals

* Survey sections that were reviewed and refined in FY 1993, FY 1994, or FY 1995.

The benchmarking project conducted for the Association for Continuing Higher Education (ACHE) primarily measured administrative processes, including noncredit course promotion, advertising, student recruitment, financial ratios on faculty and staff salaries, and the use of information technology (Alstete 1996).

If a college or university does not plan to participate in the NACUBO, or other association benchmarking projects, or if the desire for benchmarking is coming from an institution or academic unit on campus that does not have the option for an existing study, then a new benchmarking plan will be needed. Camp (1989) recommended that the best place to start is at a high strategic level and then cascade down to an individual, deliverable level. The mission statement of the organization is a good place to identify candidates for benchmarking from a strategic point of view, and the mission statement of the individual units within the organization can be useful as well. Mission statements usually identify customers, products and services, critical success factors, processes used, and more. The college or university mission statements often have very general descriptions of their objectives. For higher education, the unit level mission statements, such as those written by individual schools or departments, may be a good place to start.

Recipients of the CQI-L computer mailing list were recently asked to list activities, tasks, and subprocesses that they believed are worthy of being Benchmarked (Brigham, 1995). Ray Carlson (1995) from Dalhousie University stated that course delivery methods that reduce cost, but maintain or increase learning, should have the highest priority in benchmarking efforts; administrative processes such as registration and student advisement activities should receive lower priority. Contrary to that perception, Art Clarke from Sir Sandford Fleming College stated that administrative functions such as recruiting and registering students, although difficult, should receive top benchmarking priority. Other responses on what to benchmark include comments from a variety of different department units, with different perspectives on what processes are important. A sample of some of the other "wish lists" for benchmarking in higher education are as follows: Louise M. Illes, Brigham Young University

We are in the unique position as a university of not needing to recruit students; rather, we are forced to turn away thousands each year due [to] the nature of our being a church school. Our problems may therefore be slightly different than others. We are most interested in academic, not administrative benchmarking. The areas of highest interest for benchmarking are as follows listed by priority: General Ed curriculum, Time-to-graduation , "Major" hours requirements, Grading practices countering grade inflation, and Peer evaluation (1995, pp. 2-3).

Bruce Stark, Colorado State University

1. Quality of education received—are you able to use what was taught?
2. Percentage of students that get a job in their field within six months of graduation.
3. Diversity

4. *Quality of incoming freshmen (GPA)*
5. *Retention rates*
6. *Percentage that graduate in four years/five years* (1995,
   p. 3).
Joyce Albin, University of Oregon

*I will speak strictly for my department—which is primarily
a research and development unit, and secondarily a teaching unit . . .*

*Appropriate processes that we could benchmark might
include:*

- *Development of proposals being submitted to federal agencies and foundations*
- *Development/submission of articles to be published in
  refereed and nonrefereed journals . . .*
- *Process for finding and tracking RFP's that may be of
  interest*
- *Process for equipment purchase decisions . . .* (1995, p. 3).

The disadvantage of benchmarking at the departmental, or
"grassroots" level, is that the team, or committee of employees conducting the benchmarking, may not be able to gain
admittance to the world-class organizations needed for industry or generic benchmarking (Watson 1992). Therefore, for
maximum effectiveness benchmarking, efforts should be promoted and supported by senior level administrators, and conducted by, and for, the departmental units that will make the
most use of the information. It was the president of Oregon
State University who identified his principal customers and
the services to be provided to each customer group. The
key, critical processes identified are listed in Table 9.

These are processes identified as critical to OSU. Some
colleges and universities have already identified important
processes and have a reporting system in place that uses
key, success indices, such as the University of Miami (Sapp
& Temares 1992). Each month, the director of planning and
institutional research at Miami makes a presentation to
senior administrators on 126 indices, obtained from 18
offices throughout the university. This system is currently
used to alert senior management to problem areas and to
stimulate discussion about key sets of university information.
The information collected and presented at the University of

TABLE 9

**OSU's 12 Critical Processes
(Coate 1993, p. 10)**

Process	Performance Measure
1. Enrollment management	Concordance with enrollment management plan
2. Curriculum development	Peer acceptance
3. Teaching	Student teaching evaluation
4. International development	# of students going overseas
5. Research	Number of publications
6. Service delivery (extension) participation	% of community
7. Community relations	Number of complaints
8. Information services	Computer-student ratio
9. Long-range planning	% objectives met
10. Workforce hiring, development	% first choice hires
11. Facilities development	% of value to money for repairs
12. Funding development	$ obtained/$ requested

Miami's monthly meetings could also be used as a basis for an internal or competitive benchmarking process. Higher education has basic business processes similar to other organizations in the corporate world that can be benchmarked, and many other practices, which are somewhat unique to higher education. Potential benchmarking topics should be specific, in terms of discovering a competitive advantage, identifying the "customer," and should be interesting to others, as well. After deciding which activities to study, a blend of internal, competitive, industry, and generic benchmarking will probably be needed because of the diversity of processes found in colleges and universities.

Whom to Benchmark

We have seen that it is first necessary to decide what process or processes to benchmark. Once this is done, it then needs to be decided if it is necessary to seek the "best of the best" with generic benchmarking, or if it is more advantageous to seek a partner that is considered a "performance success" in an analogous process (Watson 1993). For institutions that are novices with benchmarking, it is recommended that more "grassroots" level studies be conducted, which measure departmental or administrative unit processes internally, or with local external competitors (Marchese 1995b). Same speed partnerships tend to return the highest value, and projects often fail when institutions reach for "too much, too soon." However, institutions that are more advanced in using quality improvement techniques will be able to get more out of benchmarking with "world-class" competitors. No matter which type of benchmarking is going to be conducted, choices have to be made about which colleges, universities, or other organizations are to be benchmarked against.

There is a proven methodology suggested by Robert Camp (1995), which seeks to identify other institutions that might become benchmarking partners, because they utilize superior processes that use best practices which could be adapted. The overall methodology for determining with whom to benchmark is to:

1. Develop a candidate list using any and all readily available information and some preliminary research.
2. Reduce the list to a target number of organizations through secondary research focused on the organization and function.
3. Prepare for a contact with the target organization and set up a visit.

Suggested places to begin searching for candidates include personal contacts, newspapers, magazines, journals, professional associations, benchmarking consultants, and the Internet. Organizations such as the American Productivity and Quality Center (APQC) in Houston, Texas, founded by companies such as AT&T, IBM, and Xerox, offer a variety of services to begin a benchmarking process, including a database of information on best practices from hundreds of companies. In addition, the APQC is planning a project in the near future focusing on higher education (Wilson 1995). Ithaca College and the University of Wisconsin have joined The Benchmarking Exchange (TBE) to obtain benchmarking partners. TBE, a California-based operation, and available via the World Wide Web, is an open service for those who wish to become members; participants do not have to join any association or special interest group in order take part (TBE 1995). TBE offers a very comprehensive and user-friendly, electronic communication and information system designed for use by individuals and organizations involved in benchmarking and process improvement. Participants can see what other organizations have done to launch their benchmarking programs, solicit help from others, contact organizations with whom to conduct a study, or even form a group with member organizations to share in a consortium-type study. The Benchmarking Exchange and The Best Practice Club—based in Bedford, UK, recently announced a strategic partnership to create a global, one-stop, on-line information and communication network dedicated to facilitating benchmarking and business excellence (TBC 1995). Additional resources for locating benchmarking partners are listed in Appendix C.

When contacting prospective benchmarking partners, it is suggested that the first communication consist of a very clear, short statement of what processes are to be benchmarked (Dale 1995). The benchmarker should demonstrate a clear understanding of what data is willing to be shared, and the opportunity and willingness to establish and maintain an ongoing dialog. The institution soliciting the benchmarking information should also have well selected and trained participants, and a good knowledge of the prospective benchmarking partner. One of the most valuable aspects of a benchmarking project, in addition to obtaining valuable information, is the creation of a new communication network between the organizations. Much of this communication may be somewhat informal, between mid-level managers who can contact each other when needed. It is this kind of communication in which best practices can be discussed, processes can be improved, and valuable inter-organizational relationships nurtured.

Data Collection
Once organizations have been chosen to analyze and benchmark, the data collection can begin. The data can be gathered internally, externally, or through original research. Most benchmarking data collection begins with internal data collection, then proceeds to publicly available secondary source data, and finally to competitive benchmarking with

external institutions. Table 10 lists potential data and information sources for higher education based on the following three categories.

Internal information can be obtained from a variety of sources, and has been shown to be productive, because it is cost-effective and can uncover additional leads to pursue. A product or service analysis of the process at another college or university is a good first step. Ordering a catalog or brochure, requesting information, and analyzing what is received can reveal valuable customer assistance information. Another place to uncover data about the organization

TABLE 10

**Information Sources
(Adapted from Camp 1989)**

Source	Example
Internal	
Library data bases	AB information
Internal reviews	Internal experts
Internal publications	Varies by organization
External	
Professional associations	AAHE, ACHE, AAUP, NACUBO
Industry publications	Chronicle of Higher Educ., Change
Special industry reports	Chronicle's Almanac
Functional trade publications	Learning Resources Network
General management	Journal of Higher Education
Seminars	By professional interest
Industry data firms	APQC, TBE
Software/hardware vendors	SCT, TRG
Advertisements	By product of interest
Newsletters	By subject matter
Original Research	
Customer feedback	Focus groups
Telephone surveys	Specific design
Inquiry service	Specific contract
Networks	Electronic, internal, and external
Consulting Firms	Educational Benchmarking Inc.

being studied is often inside the home institution. At first, it may seem unlikely that the college or university interested in obtaining the data may already have some useful information. Frequently, employees are keen observers of other organizations, or may even have been previously employed at the institution being researched. Seeking out their knowledge and assistance would be wise (Camp 1989).

The second category of public domain information includes many of the sources we have already seen, such as journals, magazines, and electronic databases. The library at the home college or university should not be overlooked as an important source for benchmarking data. In addition, library searches can be very fruitful with the use of electronic reference searches. Professional associations, consultants, and external experts, such as those discussed previously, can also yield data for reasonable rates or no cost at all. Once the categories of internal and external investigations for data have been completed, there is no choice but to proceed to the source of the best practice leader identified in the first step.

Original research can be somewhat more expensive than other approaches for data collection we have seen, but the results can be very rewarding. As in other academic or business research, it is best to approach a prospective benchmarking partner with a plan for collecting the data. A questionnaire can be useful for listing the data to be benchmarked, and it permits more extensive data gathering. Questionnaires can be completed in several ways, including mail, telephone, and in-person (Camp 1989). In the *Benchmarking Workbook*, by Gregory H. Watson (1992), many useful forms are listed, including a benchmarking questionnaire proposed for use in a study of original research. The suggested questionnaire lists the following questions to be made when contacting another organization:

1. *How do you define the process? Please describe it.*
2. *Do you consider this process to be a problem or concern in your company (college)? If not today, was it a problem in the past?*
3. *What is the measure of quality for this process? What are the criteria that you use to define excellence in process performance? How do you measure the output*

quality of this process? How do you measure progress in quality improvement?

4. *How do you consider cost and schedule in this process?*
5. *How much and what type of training do you provide for the various job categories of the process team?*
6. *What process improvements have given you the best return in performance improvements?*
7. *What company, excluding your own, do you believe is the best in performing this process?*

During their data collection state, Oregon State University's president addressed a cover letter, along with the survey form, to the president of each institution being benchmarked. A phone contact was made and instructions were also sent directly the person in the other college or university who would complete the form (Coate 1993). As in most benchmarking projects, initial contacts showed that most institutions were willing to do the considerable work necessary to complete the form, in order to receive a copy of the resulting data. Real benchmarking involves reciprocity, creating a "win-win" situation of information exchange, that is mutually beneficial (Watson 1993).

Analyzing the Benchmark Data
Once the processes to be benchmarked have been identified, the benchmarking partners are chosen, and the data collected, the next step is to determine the current competitive gap. There are three types of performance gaps: negative, parity, and positive, and are listed in Table 11 (Camp 1989). When there is a negative gap, this means that the benchmarking partner(s) have superior operational performance numbers in their processes. Examples of such numbers might include the unit cost of service being provided, the level of customer satisfaction, the financial ratio, and other such metrics we have seen in higher education benchmarking projects. If the gap is negative, a significant effort will be required to change the internal practices and process methods at the home institution to meet or exceed the external findings. The goal is to explain why the differences exist and determine the specific contributing factors or enablers. When the comparative analysis finds that the operations are at parity, or have little difference, further analysis

should be done to find the reason. If the operations of both organizations are using the most efficient method, then no changes are necessary. However, parity is no reason not to continue looking elsewhere for best practices. A positive performance gap means that the internal practices are superior to the other institutions being benchmarked. This is not to be unexpected, especially in benchmarking studies that are broad-based, and part of a consortium or association-sponsored project, such as NACUBO. Experiencing a positive gap can help a college or university maintain best

TABLE 11

**Types of Performance Gaps
(Camp 1989)**

Type	Description	Consequence
Negative	External practices superior	Benchmark based on external findings
Parity	No significant practice difference	Further analysis justified
Positive	Internal practices are superior	Benchmark based on internal findings

practices and justify the continued search for ways to close the other negative gaps which are found.

In the NACUBO benchmarking project, participants can receive a detailed gap analysis, which compares their own institution's performance with the means of all study participants and cohort groups (Table 12). The hypothetical analysis of an admissions office shows that some processes, such as departmental cost per inquiry, applicant, and matriculant are at parity (for the private research cohort), and have unfavorable gaps for other cohorts. Descriptive comments are also offered which analyze the performance. Although benchmarking data is useful, the overall goal of learning best practices will need to be completed with a site visit to the high performing institution(s).

The traditional view of college and university operational costs has been functional and organizational, and funding tends to be budgeted on the inputs of each department

TABLE 12

Gap Analysis for Cost Benchmarks - Hypothetical University's Admission Office (NACUBO 1995) (used with permission).

Results for	Departmental cost per inquiry	Departmental cost per applicant	Departmental cost per matriculant	Cost of processing a student application
Hypothetical Univ.	$56.20	$341.33	$540.05	$80.25
All Survey Participants				
Mean:	$32.34	$170.44	$494.63	$24.42
Semi-interquartile Range:	$12.84 to $26.27	$75.98 to $195.38	$193.21 to $533.30	$9.43 to $32.54
Assessment:	Significantly higher: unfavorable gap	Significantly higher; unfavorable gap	Significantly higher; unfavorable gap	Significantly higher; unfavorable gap
Public Research Cohort				
Mean:	$23.80	$109.30	$324.08	$27.51
Semi-interquartile Range:	$12.84 to $26.27	$81.38 to $115.04	$221.39 to $361.28	$9.43 to $32.54
Assessment:	Significantly higher: unfavorable gap	Significantly higher; unfavorable gap	Significantly higher; unfavorable gap	Significantly higher; unfavorable gap
Private Research Cohort				
Mean:	$32.23	$263.27	$1,231.32	$36.30
Semi-interquartile Range:	$23.13 to $60.24	$187.99 to $354.65	$459.18 to $1,209	$27.25 to $39.26
Assessment:	No Significant difference: neutral gap	No Significant difference: neutral gap	No Significant difference: neutral gap	Significantly higher; unfavorable gap
Comments on Hypothetical University's Performance	More costly than other public research universities, but in line with the overall set of institutions and the private research cohort	Higher cost than other public research institutions and overall, but once again, Hypothetical approximates the average value for the private research cohort.	More costly than both public research and overall, but on par with private research cohort.	Among the highest, least favorable values among all survey participants; significantly higher than all cohorts.

(Massey & Myerson 1994). The assumption in this strategy is that the more money that is put into a department, division, or institution, the better the quality that will result. Therefore, financial benchmarking is typically seen as input driven, and few measures of service output are usually available. Most process benchmarking efforts begin to address the need for outputs, which can help colleges and universities reshape their cost structure. Many of these are more "grassroots" efforts that are conducted by individual units within institutions. The outputs can be measured using the different types of benchmarking we have discussed. Massey and Meyerson (1994) offered an example of output benchmarking, which examines the gift processing performance, is noted in Table 13. On average, it takes 42 days to acknowledge a donor's gift to the university at a cost of $19 per transaction. If the university processes 48,000 transactions per year, and could meet the Best-in-Class gap of $10, then it could improve the responsiveness by 35 days and reduce the annual aggregate transaction costs by $480,000. This could also yield additional future donations, because the "customer" donors would be much better served.

By analyzing the benchmark data across the different benchmarking types, such as internal, competitive, industry, and generic/best-in-class, it is easy to see where the home organization truly stands in its performance against others. Benchmarking enables the practitioner to go beyond a "gut

TABLE 13

**Gift Processing - Performance Assessment
(Massey & Myerson 1994)**

Gift Acknowledgement Process	Current Performance	Customer perception	Industry bench-marking	Best-in-class bench-marking	Customer gap	Industry gap	Best-in-class gap
Response	42 days	14 days	17 days	7 days	28 days	25 days	35 days
Cost per Acknowledgment	$19	N/A	$11	$9	N/A	$8	$10

feel" that the process can be improved. It provides the data, or "pegs" of where the performance level can and should advance, both in an industry and externally. Data can be even more compelling if it is compared and analyzed using the different benchmarking types, and/or if the data is analyzed graphically. Camp (1989) and Dale (1995), offer suggestions on how benchmarking results can be graphically analyzed to reveal the performance gaps. Figures 7 and 8 show how benchmarking data, that was collected over time, can be compared with the benchmarking partners, both before and after the improvements were made. If the data being benchmarked is a process, then the vertical Y-axis value units will often show an increase in better quality, speed, or efficiency, as seen in Figure 7. If the data is for the cost of a process, then the line chart will usually attempt to show a decrease in costs relative to the benchmarking partners, as seen in Figure 8.

The performance gaps between the home institution and the competitors are easy to see. These examples are intended

FIGURE 7—Rate of Improvement Example (adapted from Dale 1995, p. 15)

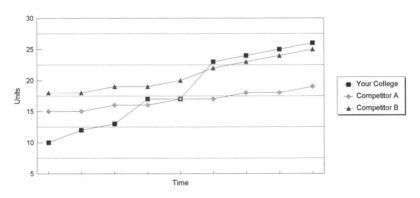

FIGURE 8—Cost Reduction Example (adapted from Dale 1995, p. 15)

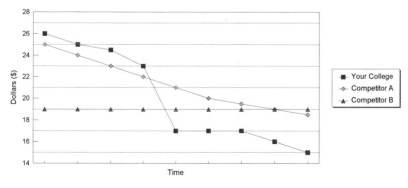

to show how benchmarking data is graphed longitudinally, with process changes (after the first benchmarking cycle) implemented at about the third or fourth time period on the X-axis. This is where the increase in quality speed or efficiency is evident in both the rate of improvement chart, and the decrease in cost reduction is shown in the cost reduction chart. When analyzing the data, one must be aware of the context in which the data was gathered. If the benchmark percentages, ratios, and other metrics were calculated by different individuals, possibly at different organizations, the researcher should consider this when reading the numbers in order to identify false performance results. A NACUBO book published before the current benchmarking era, titled *College and University Budgeting*, urges caution in the use of cost analysis with comparative data for decision-making (Meisinger & Dubeck 1984). These concerns include the notion that different colleges and universities have different sets of decision rules that are used to allocate costs to final cost centers, or even to develop direct costs. For example, compensation or salary for deans may be classified as executive management at one institution, and academic administration at another. This kind of difference can be accounted for, if the benchmarking survey form is accompanied by detailed instructions on how to calculate the benchmark ratios and data needed for the project. The current NACUBO benchmarking survey includes descriptive instructions on how to calculate the survey responses. However, one other concern noted in the 1984 report is the influence of external variables on longitudinal data. When comparing longitudinal data across institutions, changes that are observed by either the home institution or the benchmarking partners may be influenced heavily by external factors, such as shifts in student demand, and not from internal academic and management decisions. This is one reason that many benchmarking projects rely on cohort or peer groups of institutions, that may be influenced more or less equally by the environmental or external factors. Gregory Watson (1993) recommended asking a series of questions to clarify the results, including the following:

- *What is the extent of time over which the process was measured?*
- *Was there any change in the measurement system, such as the measurement tools used?*

- *How much of the measurement system relies on human observations or correlation, versus true data analysis?*
- *How are these correlations substantiated?*
- *How often or at what intervals were the measures taken?*
- *What is the estimated margin for error?*
- *Are the measures verifiable, auditable, and repeatable?* (p. 49)

After the data has been analyzed, the process enablers, which equip the high performing institution being benchmarked to achieve its status, need to be identified. An enabler can be a system, method, document, training, or other technique that facilitates the successful implementation of the benchmarked process.

Implementing Changes

Finally, after the data has been collected and analyzed, and the process enablers identified, the benchmarking efforts must be converted into actions for improving the processes which were studied. It is well known that administrators receive many reports, and often, just allow them to collect dust on a shelf. Although very interesting to college and university personnel, benchmarking results should be more than an academic exercise. Short-term and long-term goals should be established by the administrator or faculty member in charge of the project to eliminate the negative performance gaps uncovered. The short-term goals should include reducing the negative gap, and at least reaching parity, by adapting the best-practices discovered at other organizations. Long-term goals should seek to maximize the positive performance gap and become the standard by which other organizations will benchmark. Part of the long-term plan should be to integrate benchmarking into all of the vital processes within the college or university, with continual evaluation at regular intervals. Benchmarking should not be a one-time project or snapshot of a process performance, it should be ongoing (no less than quarterly) and use longitudinal data that can be charted and graphed. If benchmarking is fully integrated and implemented, then the organization will always remain current with changing market conditions (Camp 1989).

Spendolini (1992) stated there are a number of actions that should be taken during this final stage of the first

If benchmarking is fully integrated and implemented, then the organization will always remain current with changing market conditions.

benchmarking iteration. The following actions are offered in random order:

- Produce a benchmarking report/summary
- Present benchmarking findings to benchmarking customers (student, faculty, administrative units, etc.)
- Communicate findings
  —Internal—other functional groups
  —Benchmark partners
- Look for opportunities
  —Product /process improvements
  —Learning—bring new ideas and concepts into the organization
  —Forming functional networks
- Encourage recycling efforts
  —Modify/improve the use of the process
  —Introduce new/related subjects for benchmarking

The benchmarking report is intended to be delivered to the benchmarking customers, which for colleges and universities could be students, faculty, administrative units, companies that hire the graduates, state governments, and other external agencies. A summary of the data that were collected and analyzed should be included, with a record of the organizations that were benchmarked. In the corporate world, lengthy reports are becoming less common (Spendolini 1992), but benchmarking reports generated by organizations such as NACUBO can be of significant length (Kempner 1993). The report may contain the statement of need or purpose for the project, a list of the project customers, the project team, calendars of events, the subjects which were benchmarked, the information sources, methodology, results, analysis, and future actions to be taken (Spendolini 1992). In the field of higher education, which has familiarity with research methodology, it could be especially important to include a somewhat detailed report, in order for the project to gain the full respect of the college or university community it hopes to change. When the findings are presented to the benchmarking customers, both a written and oral version of the benchmarking report are suggested for maximum effectiveness. Of course, in addition to the data results and analysis, the recommendations for process improvements by the benchmarking team/committee must be communicated at this time, along with specific goals, timetables, and funding requirements to enact meaningful changes. The majority of the process improvements recommended will involve one or more of the following improvement outcomes:

- *Product/process improvements*—the primary goal, where the benchmarkers use the information collected to alter the actual processes that were analyzed.
- *Learning*—for many of the benchmarking projects reviewed for this report, one of the most common reports was that the benchmarking process was very valuable for institutional self-analysis and for seeing the college/university from an external point of view. Also, the opportunity to learn new ideas and return them to the home organization is very rewarding.
- *Forming functional networks*—Often, an unexpected outcome and by-product occurs when the benchmarking participants establish valuable contacts at other institutions, whom they can call for information about benchmarking or non-benchmarking related improvement activities.

As stated earlier, for the benchmarking process to be fully effective, it needs to be recycled or recalibrated, and the data has to be measured over time. Often, benchmarking practitioners become more proficient in their use of the process, and will diagnose their own individual process strengths and weaknesses, and adjust their benchmarking behaviors accordingly (Spendolini 1992). In addition, new subjects for benchmarking are often added or deleted in subsequent years of the project, as is the case with NACUBO (NACUBO 1995).

Aside from the overall benchmarking report, Gregory Watson (1992) suggested the creation of an action plan for implementing each individual process enabler. This action plan can follow the general format of a Japanese *hoshin* plan, which he defines as "a system for establishing process objectives and goals and implementing them through a set of strategies, that are monitored at particular milestones to determine if the process is on target" (p. 92). Breakthrough improvements can be readily identified if a significant gap in performance is seen in the critical success factors of the key processes being studied. For each process, a process "owner" should be identified,who will have responsibility for the process functions and work activities. The owner can be an individual or group within the institution, who will oversee the efficiency, effectiveness, and economy of the process by eliminating waste and implementing the improvements. To help the process owner build the action plan, the form is outlined in Figure 9, which identifies the key process and critical success factor for each improvement being implemented. The form begins by listing the key process being measured and the critical success factor for the process. Next, the date that the action plan is written and the summary of the benchmarking study results are entered. Under objective, there should be the recorded actual changes that this action plan will accomplish, the expected date of completion, and the performance level of the critical success factor which is sought. The short-term goals are typically six months to one year in length, and long-term goals should have an expected date of achievement. The benchmark, or peg, against which this process is measured, is recorded with the date of the observation, the institution's name, level, and rate of performance. The last section of the form lists specific strategies required for achieving the changes, along with the name of the owner responsible for completion. Each of the strategies should have targets and milestones for the performance. A previous section showed that graphically monitoring process performance can be a very useful part of reinforcing the benchmarking goals. The data from the action plan can be used in conjunction with the performance charts to set realistic and achievable performance goals.

As with any organizational improvement technique, there is the possibility that action taken on the benchmarking project will not be successful. One proven way to avoid this is to study the causes of failure found by others and take steps not to repeat them.

The American Productivity and Quality Center conducted a research study on the causes of benchmarking project failures. Survey respondents were asked to rate factors identified for failure on a five-point scale (5 = high cause) to indicate the significance of the factor's contribution to an unsuccessful benchmarking study. Multiple answers to the survey question were not allowed. The results are listed as follows:

FIGURE 9—Benchmarking Action Plan (adapted from Watson 1992, p. 92)

Process: _____ _____ Critical Success Factor: _____ _____ Process Owner: _____ Date: _____	
Summary of the Study Results	
Objective _____ _____ Benchmark Institution: _____ Date Observed: _____ Level _____	Goals Short-term Long-Term Rate: _____
Strategy (owner) _____	Targets and Milestones

The top four causes of benchmarking project failure were poor planning, no-top management support, no process-owner involved, and insufficient benchmarking skills. All four of these problems can be addressed by colleges and universities that plan to conduct a project, and have been discussed earlier in the review of the benchmarking litera-

TABLE 14

**Causes of Benchmarking Study Failures
(APQC 1993, p. 131)**

Question	Rating (1-5)
Poor planning	3.78
No top management support	3.76
No process owner involved	3.56
Insufficient benchmarking skills	3.54
Low priority	3.14
Results not believed	2.93
Lack of interest	2.76
Lack of funding	2.68
Poor teamwork	2.67
Personnel turnover	2.20
No better practices found	2.17
Interpersonal conflicts	2.07

ture and its application to higher education. Proper project planning, support from the president's office and the "grass-roots" units where the efforts should take place, and proper employee training are important for all organizational improvements.

Benchmarking Software

Due to its reliance on stepwise methodology, computer software has been developed for conducting a benchmarking project. Recently, data was submitted electronically for the 1995 fiscal year NACUBO project, in order to increase speed of data collection and to facilitate data integrity (NACUBO 1995). The benchmarking software is provided to the participants on a Microsoft Excel™ spreadsheet, and all participants receive a complementary educational version of the software. There is also available, at least one general computer software package, which is specifically designed to help simplify a benchmarking project at any organization. LearnerFirst's *Benchmarking* software was developed in a joint venture with the American Society for Quality Control (ASQC 1995). This software application breaks the benchmarking process into simple, step-by-step activities to conduct successful benchmarking projects for both beginners and experienced benchmarkers. It is an interactive Windows™ application that provides the user with specific examples, dialogue questions, suggestions, guidelines, and checklists that help carry out consistent and effective benchmarking projects (ASTM 1995). The software was adapted from the methodology of benchmarking expert H. James Harrington, president of the International Academy for Quality and the international quality advisor for Ernst & Young. The interface and illustrations allow for quick and highly-interactive navigation through an entire benchmarking process, in 19 detailed steps or activities:

1. *Identify what to benchmark*
2. *Obtain management support*
3. *Develop measurements*
4. *Develop the data collection plan*
5. *Review plans with location experts*
6. *Characterize your benchmark team*
7. *Collect internal published information*
8. *Select internal benchmarking sites*
9. *Collect internal original research*
10. *Conduct interview and surveys*
11. *Form benchmarking committee*
12. *Conduct internal site visits*
13. *Collect external published information*
14. *Conduct external original research*
15. *Identify corrective actions*
16. *Develop an implementation plan*
17. *Gain approval of implementation plan*
18. *Implement changes and measure impact*
19. *Maintain a database* (ASTM 1995, p. 2-3)

This approach follows and expands upon the multi-step benchmarking processes that were reviewed in the second chapter, and could provide a useful framework tool for college and university personnel who plan to conduct a benchmarking project. The package currently sells for $475, and is distributed by ASTM, 100 Barr Harbor Drive, West Conshohocken, PA 19428-2959. Professor Charles Barclay (1995) at the University of Hawaii reported that the software has also been successfully used in a graduate business program curriculum, and that class benchmarking projects are required of students in the Production and Operations Management and the Business Strategy courses.

Conclusion

More than 20 years ago, Martin Trow (1973) wrote about the tremendous growth in higher education, and the variety of problems it creates for higher education in areas such as curriculum, finance, government and administration. He believes that many of the current problems are actually a related cluster of difficulties arising out of what he calls the transition from elite, to mass, to universal higher education. The different phases are associated with different functions of higher education, for students and society at large. Under the current phase of "universal higher education," when more than 50 percent of the students of eligible age attend college at some point, Trow stated that management procedures become more dependent on quantified data for the assessment of costs and benefits. One method of quantifying the cost and other data now available and being used by higher education is benchmarking. However, benchmarking does more than quantify the costs and benefits. It enables the organization to learn, and continue to learn, best practices for improving its operations, whether the improvements are in the teaching of undergraduate or graduate programs, research, or college and university administration.

This report has reviewed the origins of the benchmarking process, examined its use in higher education today, and provided instruction on how to begin a project to compare and improve an institution of higher education. It is important to understand the different types of benchmarking discussed in the second chapter and to know that some approaches to benchmarking are more appropriate than others. For example, some benchmarking practitioners believe that it is always necessary to compare their institution only with world-class organizations, or else the improvement goals will be too easy (Thor 1995). They believe that benchmarking is to be used only for obtaining at least a tenfold increase in productivity, and that a mere doubling of performance is not sufficient. There are several problems with this fear of "cohort mediocrity," as one benchmarking consultant labeled it (Dale 1995). First, no organization is world-class in all areas, only institutional practices, processes, and approaches are world-class. It is possible to find a benchmarking partner that may not be well-known for overall quality, but may be very good at the process that is being sought for improvement. In addition, if a true world-class best practitioner can be found, it may be difficult or impossible to arrange a benchmarking site visit because of the competition to get the same information. Less waiting time is often available at other institutions, which, although not as well known, can offer useful improvement strategies. Quick response to the rapidly changing competitive environment can be critical for success, especially in the "nanosecond nineties" (Peters 1992).

Kinni (1994) stated that there are a few lessons that consistently occur in the literature on benchmarking:

- *Benchmarking is not a profit center. Understand its uses and pull it from the toolbox only when it is the best tool for the job.*
- *Start by benchmarking functions or processes that are critical to success. Don't waste time or money on insignificant studies.*
- *Benchmarking requires self-assessment. You cannot uncover performance gaps without first understanding and measuring your own processes.*
- *Gather the most cost-effectiveness information first. The more you learn before an on-site visit, the more you will take away from it.*
- *Implement, implement, implement! Without implementation, a benchmarking study is an academic exercise of no value* (p. 28).

Other recurring themes in the benchmarking literature include the idea that benchmarking is fundamentally a learning behavior by the institution, and that proper planning is required for a successful benchmarking effort. Colleges and universities must realize that they, like all organizations, do not perform all, or even most, of the functional processes best. For each process performed, there are leaders who are the best in a cohort group, best in industry, and best-in-class. Benchmarking is the identification of metrics, or common measures and measurement techniques, to determine who is the best, and the application of these techniques to organizational processes (Losh 1994). It is critical that benchmarking partners use the same metrics, because no comparative analysis can be made on unlike data. For benchmarking to be truly effective, it is important to use the metrics to make changes and then reassess the improvements after the changes are made, in order to measure the performance improvement. Simply obtaining the measures without action is a waste of time and money for the college or university.

The literature reviewed on benchmarking in higher education tends to be very process oriented, and usually not strategic in its use by colleges and universities. While it is good advice for institutions that are beginning to use benchmarking to start out with small projects and then proceed to benchmark broader areas of coverage, a broader use of this tool beyond the functional process level and into strategic planning and goal-setting can be very helpful, as colleges and universities seek to position themselves competitively in the new information society. Today, institutions of higher education are discovering that they can no longer attempt to follow Ezra Cornell's vision to "found an institution where any person can find instruction in any study" (Veysey 1965). Increasing competition, the information explosion, and changing student needs have made it unwise for institutions to lack focus and specialization. In his book titled *Strategic Benchmarking*, Watson (1993) stated that strategic benchmarking involves the application of process benchmarking techniques to the development of a greater understanding of strategic issues, by forming cooperative alliances with other organizations. Based on Watson's suggestions for all types of organizations, and other literature on the concerns in higher education, issues that could be addressed by strategic benchmarking in higher education include:

- Building core competencies that will help sustain competitive advantage
- Targeting a specific shift in strategy, such as entering new educational markets or new educational programs
- Developing a new service or making a strategic acquisition
- Creating an institution that is more capable of learning how to respond in [an] uncertain future because it has increased its acceptance to change.

Strategic benchmarking for colleges and universities should be closely linked to the strategic planning process. The benchmarking studies which are conducted could address specific issues in the plan, such as the establishment of goals and objectives, development of the institutional infrastructure, selection of key functional processes for improvement, identification of technology areas for development, etc. (Watson 1993). The college or university president and senior staff should set the breadth of the strategic benchmarking study, and the methodology can be similar to the process benchmarking discussed.

Benchmarking is not a remedy for all of the problems that face higher education in the 1990s; it is only one of many practical approaches to improving organizational quality and reassessing how resources are spent (Rush 1994). Other tools such as committee studies, "task force" white papers, and further studies only delay the organization from the final goal of making well-planned changes. Another concern is that benchmarking requires an underlay of experience in quality management, which many colleges and universities do not yet have. Benchmarking requires the understanding of terms such as teams, processes, customers, metrics, outputs, and others that may seem daunting and unfamiliar to untrained personnel. Marchese (1995) stated that like TQM itself, the practice of benchmarking has a threshold barrier, because it does require extra effort to begin and sustain a project. Business corporations, health care organizations, and others have tended to be pressured for improvement efforts more profoundly than institutions of higher education, where the sense of felt need and urgency for improvement is relatively low. Despite these concerns, benchmarking offers the potential to teach institutions of higher education how external perspectives, on organizational processes, can enrich internal values. When combined with TQM, BPR, and continuous quality improvement, benchmarking is a potent vehicle for promoting substantive change-oriented action because of its reliance on hard data from external comparisons. Benchmarking blends with the entire quality improvement process (Dale 1995). TQM is the underpinning, holistic approach that includes benchmarking. Business process reengineering is the natural result of benchmarking, as a successful benchmarking project determines that the process being examined needs to be changed. Wheaton College learned how to integrate bench-marking with TQM and BPR efforts, and help bring about significant improvements, build staff skills, and begin a revolution in the way staff approach their work (Kempner 1993). Wheaton sought to use TQM for customer focus and staff involvement, BPR for rapid results, and benchmarking to ensure that both TQM and BPR address areas of greatest potential and to avoid repeating past mistakes. Edwin J. Merck, Wheaton's vice president for finance and operations, added:

> *Benchmarking really gives more power to our TQM and BPR efforts. Continuous improvement could be pursued within our own environment exclusively, but benchmarking has helped us dovetail with other improvement processes at other places. It introduces ideas we might [have] never thought of, and it keeps us more competitive* (Kempner 1993, p. 30).

Although Wheaton participates in a professional association study (NACUBO), benchmarking can also help an organization continue to learn how to improve, if it is done individually, or through a consortium or professional association.

Twenty years ago, it would be unheard of for Carnegie Mellon University to improve the campus renovations process by partnering with the Eastman Kodak Company (Nicklin 1995). Benchmarking allows institutions to break out of the old way of doing things, such as using an intuition-based, or "gut-feeling," approach to business process analysis. Looking at a process,and deciding without knowing why it is done that way, or rationalizing it by saying, "it's always been done like that," is an excuse that is too common for not making improvements. Ken Bardach, MBA Program Director at Michigan State University, stated that "Benchmarking forces us to do the things that good managers want to do, but find excuses not to do . . . It forces us to put mirrors around us, look at what we're doing, and see if we're doing it well" (AACSB 1994, p. 17). The "new paradigm" that is fast approaching, and already here for many institutions, requires that we build efficiency into the basic structure and functioning of the organization (Keeton & Mayo-Wells 1994). Part of this new pattern is that today, higher education must continually improve, just as individuals in society must pursue lifelong learning. If learning is to be the main focus, and students are now using technology continually to receive training at home or at the worksite, then it is vital that colleges and universities keep up with the competition by continually comparing and improving with new tools such as benchmarking.

APPENDIX A—BALDRIGE AWARD 1995 EDUCATION CRITERIA ITEM LISTING (SEYMOUR 1996, PP. 318 & 321)

	Point Values
1.0 Leadership	**90**
1.1 Senior Administration Leadership	40
1.2 Leadership System and Organization	30
1.3 Public Responsibility and Citizenship	20
2.0 Information and Analysis	**75**
2.1 Management of Information and Data	25
2.2 Comparisons and Benchmarking	15
2.3 Analysis and Use of Institution-Level Data	35
3.0 Strategic and Operational Planning	**75**
3.1 Strategy Development	45
3.2 Strategy Deployment	30
4.0 Human Resource Development and Management	**150**
4.1 Human Resource Planning and Evaluation	30
4.2 Faculty and Staff Work Systems	30
4.3 Faculty and Staff Development	50
4.4 Faculty and Staff Well-Being and Satisfaction	40
5.0 Educational and Business Process Management	**150**
5.1 Education Design	40
5.2 Education Delivery	25
5.3 Education Support Service Design and Delivery	25
5.4 Research, Scholarship, and Service	20
5.5 Enrollment Management	20
5.6 Business Operations Management	20
6.0 Institutional Performance Results	**230**
6.1 Student Performance Results	100
6.2 Education Climate Improvement Results	50
6.3 Research, Scholarship, and Service Results	40
6.4 Business Performance Results	40
7.0 Student Focus and Student and Stakeholder Satisfaction	**230**
7.1 Current Student Needs and Expectations	40
7.2 Future Student Needs and Expectations	30
7.3 Stakeholder Relationship Management	40
7.4 Student & Stakeholder Satisfaction Determination	30
7.5 Student and Stakeholder Satisfaction Results	50
7.6 Student and Stakeholder Satisfaction Comparison	40
TOTAL POINTS	**1000**

Selected Baldrige Award criteria descriptions requiring benchmarking:

2.2 Comparisons and Benchmarking *(15pts.)*

Describe the institution s processes for selecting and using comparative information and data to support overall college or university performance improvement.

Areas to Address

a. How comparisons and benchmarking information and data are selected and used to help drive improvement of overall institutional performance. Describe: (1) how needs and priorities are determined; (2) criteria for seeking appropriate information and data—from within and outside the academic community; (3) how the benchmarking information and data are used within the institution to improve understanding of processes and process performance; and (4) how the information and data are used to set improvement targets and/or encourage breakthrough approaches.
b. How the institution evaluates and improves its overall process for selecting and using comparisons and benchmarking information and data to improve planning and overall college or university performance.

6.0 Institution Performance Results *(230 pts.)*

The Institution Performance Results Category examines student performance and improvement, improvement in the institution's education climate and institutional services, and improvement in performance of business operations. Also examined are performance levels relative to comparable institutions and/or appropriately selected organizations.

6.1 Student Performance Results *(100 pts.)*

Summarize results of improvement in student performance using key measures and/or indicators of such performance.

Areas to Address

a. current levels and trends in key measures and/or indicators of student performance.
b. for results presented in 6.1a, demonstrate that there has been improvement in student performance.
c. For the results in 6.1a, show how student performance and performance trends compare with comparable institutions and/or comparable student populations.

APPENDIX B—THE BENCHMARKING CODE OF CONDUCT

(from the Benchmarking Management Guide, published by the American Productivity and Quality Center, (APQC 1993, p. 229).

Preamble

Benchmarking—the process of identifying and learning from best practices anywhere in the world—is a powerful tool in the quest for continuous improvement.

To guide benchmarking encounters and to advance the professionalism and effectiveness of benchmarking, the International Benchmarking Clearinghouse, a service of the American Productivity and Quality Center, and the Strategic Planning Institute Council on Benchmarking have adopted this common Code of Conduct. We encourage all organizations to abide by this Code of Conduct. Adherence to these principles will contribute to efficient, effective, and ethical benchmarking. This edition of the Code of Conduct has been expanded to provide greater guidance on the protocol of benchmarking for beginners.

The Benchmarking Code of Conduct

Individuals agree for themselves and their company to abide by the following principles for benchmarking with other organizations.

1. *Principle of Legality*
- If there is any potential question on the legality of an activity, don't do it.
- Avoid discussions or actions that could lead to or imply an interest in restraint of trade, market, and/or customer allocation schemes, price fixing, dealing arrangements, bid rigging, or bribery. Don't discuss costs with competitors if costs are an element of pricing.
- Refrain from the acquisition of trade secrets from any means that could be interpreted as improper, including the breach or inducement of a breach of duty to maintain secrecy. Do not disclose or use any trade secret that may have been obtained through improper means, or that was disclosed by another in violation of a duty to maintain its secrecy or limit its use.
- Do not, as a consultant or a client, extend one benchmarking study's findings to another company without first obtaining permission from the parties of the study.

2. *Principle of Exchange*
- Be willing to provide the same type and level of information that you request from your benchmarking partner to your benchmarking partner.
- Communicate fully and early in the relationship to clarify expectations, avoid misunderstandings, and establish mutual interest in the benchmarking exchange.
- Be honest and complete.

3. *Principle of Confidentiality*
- Treat benchmarking interchange as confidential to the individuals and companies involved. Information must not be communicated outside the partnering organizations without the prior consent of the benchmarking partner who shared the information.
- An organization s participation in a study is confidential and should not be communicated externally without its prior participation.

4. *Principle of Use*
- Use information obtained through benchmarking only for purposes of formulating improvement of operations or processes within the companies participating in the benchmarking study.
  The use or communication of a benchmarking partner's name with the data obtained, or practices observed requires the prior permission of that partner.
  Do not use benchmarking as a means to market or sell.

5. *Principle of First-Party Contact*
- Initiate benchmarking contacts, whenever possible, through a benchmarking contact designated by the partner organization.
- Respect the organizational culture of partner organizations and work within mutually agreed upon procedures.
- Obtain mutual agreement with the designated benchmarking contact on any hand-off of communication, or responsibility to the other parties.

6. *Principle of Third-Party Contact*
- Obtain an individual's permission before providing his or her name in response to a contact request.

- Avoid communicating a contact's name in an open forum without the contact s permission.

7. *Principle of Preparation*
- Demonstrate commitment to the efficiency and effectiveness of benchmarking by completing preparatory work prior to making an initial benchmarking contact, and following a benchmarking process.
- Make the most of your benchmarking partners' time by being fully prepared for each exchange.
- Help you benchmarking partners prepare by providing them with an interview guide or questionnaire and agenda, prior to benchmarking visits.

8. *Principle of Completion*
- Follow through with each commitment made to your benchmarking partners in a timely manner.
- Complete each benchmarking study to the satisfaction of all benchmarking partners as mutually agreed.

9. *Principle of Understanding and Action*
- Understanding how your benchmarking partners would like to be treated.
- Treat your benchmarking partners in the way that each benchmarking partner would like to be treated.

APPENDIX C—BENCHMARKING RESOURCES

When conducting a benchmarking project, it is important to search thoroughly for information on other institutions that are reported as high performing in the process(es) which are being analyzed. In addition to the traditional ERIC service, and the books and articles cited in this report, there are other useful sources of primary and secondary information for institutions of higher education, such as:

- Academe Today—A complimentary service reserved for subscribers to the Chronicle of Higher Education provides statistics, reports, and the past five years of articles from the Chronicle, which are searchable and available for full-text reading or downloading. The World-Wide Web address is: http://chronicle.com
- AERA Listservs—The American Educational Research Association sponsors 14 Listservs on the Internet. There are two general Lists, 11 Division lists and a list for graduate students. AERA-J Division J is for postsecondary education. All Lists reside at the Internet address LISTSERV@ASUACAD.BITNET which is at Arizona State University.
- AskERIC Virtual Library—This is one of the best education sites available via the Internet, and allows access to the Department of Education's ERIC Database. The Internet address is: http://ericir.syr.edu
- BPRREENG-L—This Listserv was created in mid-April 1995, and tries to facilitate the development of a human network consisting of members with shared interests and skills in the field. Its purpose is to promote a constructive dialogue about college and university related Business Process Reengineering-related information. The Internet address is: LISTSERVER@LISTS.ACS.OHIO-STATE.EDU
- CQI-L Listserv—This Listserv provides a moderated forum for all individuals interested in the principles and practices of Continuous Quality Improvement and its application to the improvement of higher education. It is sponsored by the American Association for Higher Education, and it is available at the following Internet address: CQI-L@MR.NET
- Educational Benchmarking Inc. (EBI)—This is a private consulting company formed by Joe Pica, assistant dean and MBA program director at Indiana University, and

Glenn Detrick, an educational consultant. They work with the Graduate Management Admission Council and the American Assembly of Collegiate Schools of Business on various benchmarking projects for undergraduate and graduate business education.

- HEPROC Assessment Home Page—These archives address many areas of assessment in higher education, including summative, formative, student self-assessment, institutional self-assessment, mandates, classroom assessment techniques, and other useful services including the HEPROC-L and the CQI-L Archive. The Internet address is: http://pobox.com/~higher.education

- International Benchmarking Clearinghouse (IBC), a division of the American Productivity and Quality Center (APQC)—provides a variety of products and services for benchmarking, including consultants, training and advisory services, publications, a database, case studies, and best practices classified by key work processes. Membership information is available free. American Productivity and Quality Center, 123 North Post Oak Lane, 3rd Floor, Houstan, TX 77024-7797; telephone 800-776-9676; or via the Internet World-Wide Web at: http://www.apqc.org

- NACUBO's Benchmarking Process for Improvement in Higher Education. Conducted annually with the assistance of Cooper's & Lybrand, L.L.P., Barbara S. Shafer & Associates, John Minter Associates, and Sterling Research/Sutton Associates. For further information or a prospectus, contact the National Association of College and University Business Officers, One Dupont Circle, Suite 500, Washington, DC 20036-1178.

- National Cooperative Data Share - Benchmark Data Exchange, by John Minter Associates, Inc., is a subscription service offering immediate access to higher education benchmarks produced by participating institutions. Institutions may participate in categories of their choosing, such as revenue, expenditures, balance sheet, gains and losses, faculty, undergraduate and graduate enrollment, graduation, retention, staff, and student services cost centers. This service is currently available on the World Wide Web at http://www.edmin.com/jma.ncds.html

- Society for College and University Planning (SCUP) links

to higher education resources—A very useful page containing World-Wide Web starting places for on-line research, news periodicals, higher education periodicals, speeches/statements, departments of higher education, planning, physical plants, etc., and other higher education associations. Internet address: http://www-personal.umich.edu/~scup/ LINKS.html

- The Benchmarking Exchange (TBE)—This information system is designed specifically for use by individuals and organizations involved in benchmarking and process improvement. TBE provides users with a comprehensive, centralized, and specialized forum for all phases of benchmarking. Several colleges and universities are currently listed as members. The Internet World Wide Address is: http://www.benchnet.com

- U.S. Department of Education Web Server, a comprehensive resource for educators which contains goals, inititiatives, news, press releases, funding opportunities, and official documents of the agency, including hypertext publications. Useful resources include the Education Department's Teacher's and Researcher's Guides. The Internet address is: http://www.ed.gov

REFERENCES

AACSB. (1994). New Benchmarking Survey Makes Business Schools Introspective. *Newsline*, 25(1), 16-17.

AAHE. (1994). *CQI 101: A First Reader for Higher Education* (CQ9401). Washington, DC: American Association for Higher Education.

AIR. (1994, May 28-June 1, 1994). *NACUBO Benchmarking*. Paper presented at the 34th Annual Forum of the Association for Institutional Research, New Orleans, LA.

Albin, L. M. (1995). Benchmarking: Wish Lists/Benchmarkability (p. 3). HEPROC CQI-L

Archive: American Association for Higher Education.

Alstete, J. W. (1994). Benchmarking and Continuous Improvement at Seton Hall. Journal of the National Association of Graduate Admission Professionals, 6(1), 1-3.

Alstete, J. W. (1996). A Competitive Benchmarking Study of Non-Credit Program Administration. The *Journal of Continuing Higher Education*, 44(2), 23-33.

Apps, J. W. (1988). *Higher education in learning society: Meeting new demands for education and training*. San Francisco, CA: Jossey -Bass.

APQC. (1993). *The Benchmarking Management Guide - American Productivity and Quality Center*. Portland, OR: Productivity Press.

Aronow, I. (1993, January 26, 1993). Iona Closing its Campus in Yonkers. *The New York Times*, pp. sec. WC p. 9 c. 1.

ASQC. (1995). ASQC - The Quality Source. http://www.asqc.org/contact.html: American Society for Quality Control.

ASTM. (1995). Quality Control (pp. 1-5). http://www.astm.org/PUB/qualityc.html: ASTM.

Barclay, C. (1995). LearnerFirst's Benchmarking Software (pp. 1-2). QUALITY List Editor: DejaNews.

Barr, R. B., & Tagg, J. (1995). From Teaching to Learning—A New Paradigm for Undergraduate Education. Change, 27(6), 13-25.

Bateman, G. R. (1994, September 22-23, 1994). *Benchmarking and Management Education Teaching and Curriculum*. Paper presented at the American Assembly of Collegiate Schools of Business Continuous Improvement Symposium, St. Louis, MO.

Bell, D. (1973). *The Coming of the Post-Industrial Society: A Venture in Social Forecasting*. New York: Basic Books, Inc.

Birnbaum, R. (1988). How Colleges Work: The Cybernetics of Academic Organization and Leadership. San Francisco: Jossey-Bass.

Birnbaum, R. (1992). The Constraints on Campus Productivity. In R. E. Anderson & J. W. Meyerson (Eds.), *Productivity and Higher Education* (pp. 23-47). Princeton: Peterson's Guides.

Blumenstyk, G. (1995, September 1, 1993). Measuring Productivity and Efficiency: Project Aims to Come Up With Comparative Costs for Operations, From Parking To Purchasing. *The Chronicle of Higher Education*, pp. A41.

Bogan, C. E., & English, M. J. Benchmarking for Best Practices. In Brewer, P. B., Hale, C. D., & McLaurin, S. (1996). Benchmarking Academic Credit and Noncredit Continuing Education. *The Journal of Continuing Higher Education, 44*(1), p. 3.

Bosworth, K., & Hamilton, S. J. (Eds.). (1994). *Collaborative Learning: Underlying Processes and Effective Techniques.* (Vol. 59). San Francisco: Jossey-Bass.

Bowen, H. R. (1981). Cost Differences: The Amazing Disparity Among Institutions of Higher Education and Educational Costs Per Student. Change, 21-27.

Bowen, H. R., & Schuster, J. H. (1986). *American Professors: A National Resource Imperiled.* New York: Oxford University Press.

Boyer, E. L. (1990). Scholarship Reconsidered: Priorities of the Professoriate. Princeton: The Carnegie Foundation for the Advancement of Teaching.

Breedin, B. (1994). Remembering the G.I. Bill. AAHE Bulletin, 46(9), 12-13.

Brewer, P. B., Hale, C. D., & McLaurin, S. (1996). Benchmarking Academic Credit and Noncredit Continuing Education. *The Journal of Continuing Higher Education, 44*(1), 2-11.

Brigham, S. (1995). Benchmarking . HEPROC CQI-L Archive: American Association for Higher Education.

Bruffee, K. A. (1993). *Collaborative Learning: Higher Education, Interdependence, and the Authority of Knowledge.* Baltimore: Johns Hopkins University Press.

Camp, R. C. (1989). *Benchmarking: The Search for Industry Best Practices That Lead to Superior Performance.* Milwaukee, WI: ASQC Quality Press.

Camp, R. C. (1992). Learning From The Best Leads To Superior Performance. *Journal of Business Strategy*, 13(3), 3-6.

Camp, R. C. (1995). *Business Process Benchmarking: Finding and Implementing Best Practices.* Milwaukee, WI: Quality Press.

Carlson, R. (1995). Benchmarking on Campus (pp. 7). HEPROC CQI-L Archive: American Association for Higher Education.

Chaffee, E. E., & Sherr, L. A. (1992). *Quality: Transforming*

Postsecondary Education. ASHE-ERIC Higher Education Report No. 3. Washington, DC: The George Washington University, School of Education and Human Development.

Christianson, R. (1995). Problems with Benchmarking. HEPROC CQI-L Archive: American Association for Higher Education.

Clark, K. L. (1993, December 5, 1993). *Benchmarking as a Global Strategy for Improving Instruction in Higher Education.* Paper presented at the International Conference on New Concepts in Higher Education, Phoenix AZ.

Clarke, A. (1995). Benchmarking on Campuses (pp. 5). HEPROC CQI-L Archive: American Association for Higher Education.

Clotfelter, C. T., Ehrenberg, R. G., Getz, M., & Siegfried, J. J. (1991). *Economic Challenges in Higher Education.* Chicago: The University of Chicago Press.

Coate, L. E. (1992). *Reshaping the University: Restructuring and Process Re-engineering* (Unpublished Report): Oregon State University.

Coate, L. E. (1993, January 7-9). *Implementing TQM at OSU.* Paper presented at the MBA Managers Program, Rancho Santa Fe, CA.

Dale, B. (1995, October 30 & 31, 1995). *Practical Benchmarking for Colleges and Universities.* Paper presented at the AAHE Workshop, Key Biscayne, FL.

Detrick, G., Magelli, P., & Pica, J. (1994). *Benchmarking: A Key to Successful Program Review.* Paper presented at the 1994 Annual Meeting of the Graduate Management Admission Council, San Diego, CA.

Detrick, G., & Pica, J. A. (1995, April 10-12, 1995). *Benchmarking Business School Performance: Lessons Learned.* Paper presented at the American Association of Collegiate Schools of Business, Minneapolis, MN.

Dossey-Terrell, J. (1995). Benchmarking on Campuses (pp. 4). HEPROC CQI-L Archive: American Association for Higher Education.

Entin, D. H. (1994). A second look: TQM in 10 Boston-area colleges, one year later. *AAHE Bulletin, 46*(9), 3-7.

Ford, D. J. (1993). Benchmarking HRD. *Training and Development, 46*(6), 36-41.

Gaither, G., Nedwek, B. P., & Neal, J. E. (1994). *Measuring Up: The Promises and Pitfalls of Performance Indicators in Higher Education.* Washington, DC: The George Washington University.

Gardiner, L. F. (1994). Redesigning Higher Education: Producing Dramatic Gains in Student Learning. ASHE-ERIC Higher Education Report No. 7. Washington, DC: The George

Washington University, School of Education and Human Development.

Hammer, M., & Champy, J. (1993). *Reengineering the Corporation: A Manifesto for the Business Revolution.* New York: HarperCollins.

HBS. (1993). *External Comparisons Summary Report: MBA: Leadership & Learning* (N1-193-149). Boston: Harvard Business School.

Heverly, M. A., & Connesky, R. A. (1992). Total Quality Management: Increasing Productivity and Decreasing Costs. *New Directions for Institutional Research, 75,*103-114.

Hobbs, W. C. (1994). Quality and Higher Education. *Journal of Higher Education Management, 9*(2).

Illes, L. M. (1995). Benchmarking: Wish Lists/Benchmarkability (pp. 2-3). HEPROC CQI-L Archive: American Association for Higher Education.

Inger, M. (1993). *Benchmarking in Education: Tech Prep, A Case in Point.* New York: Columbia University. National Center for Research in Vocational Education, Berkeley, CA.

Jackson, N. (1995). Higher Education Benchmarking (Vol. Digest 107, pp. 1). BPREENG-L.

Jellema, W. W., & Oliver, J. (1975). *Cost of Instruction: Study of Higher Education in Indiana.* Indianapolis: Associated Colleges of Indiana.

Keeton, M., & Mayo-Wells, B. (1994). Benchmarking for Efficiency in Learning. *AAHE Bulletin, 46*(8), 9-13.

Keller, G. (1983). *Academic Strategy: The Management Revolution in American Higher Education.* Baltimore: The Johns Hopkins University Press.

Kempner, D. E. (1993). The Pilot Years: The Growth of the NACUBO Benchmarking Project. *NACUBO Business Officer, 27*(6), 21-31.

Kerridge, D. (1995). Continuous Quality Improvement Issues in Higher Education. In S. Brigham (Ed.), *Problems with Benchmarking.* cqi-l@MR.Net: American Association of Higher Education.

Kimmerling, G. (1993). Gathering Best Practices. *Training and Development,* 47(9), 28-32.

Kinni, T. B. (1994, December 5, 1994). Measuring Up. *Industry Week,* 27-28.

Leibfried, K. H. J., & McNair, C. J. (1992). *Benchmarking.* New York: Harper Collings Publishers.

LERN. (1992). *Ratios for Success* (304). Manhattan, KS: Learning

Resources Network.

Losh, C. (1994). Benchmarking Technical Education Delivery Systems. *Vocational Education Journal, 69*(7), 62.

Marchese, T. (1991). TQM Reaches the Academy. *AAHE Bulletin, 44*(3), 3-9.

Marchese, T. (1994, January/February). Getting the Baldrige Right. *Change, 26*, 4.

Marchese, T. (1995a, July/August). The Management of Colleges. *Change, 27*, 1.

Marchese, T. (1995b). Understanding Benchmarking. *AAHE Bulletin, 47*(8), 3-5.

Martin, D. (1995, May 14, 1995). Upsala Ceremony is a Last Hurrah. *The New York Times*, pp. Sec. B, p. 5, c. 1.

Massey, W. F., & Myerson, J. (Eds.). (1994). *Measuring Institutional Performance in Higher Education*. Princeton, NJ: Peterson's Guides.

McMillen, L. (1990, September 5, 1990). Study Finds Colleges Spend About 16 Cents to Raise Dollar. *The Chronicle of Higher Education*, pp. A31.

Meisinger, R. J., Jr., & Dubeck, L. W. (1984). *College and University Budgeting: An Introduction for Faculty and Academic Administrators*. Washington, DC: National Association of College and University Business Officers.

Middaugh, M. (1995). Telephone Conversation.

Middaugh, M. F., & Hollowell, D. E. (1992). Examining Academic and Administrative Productivity measures. *New Directions For Institutional Research*, 75, 61-76.

Minter, J. M. (1996). *National Cooperative Data Share - Benchmark Data Exchange*. Available on the internet at http://www.edmin.com/jma/ncds.html

NACUBO. (1995). *Benchmarking Prospectus*. Washington, DC: National Association of College and University Business Officers.

Naisbitt, J. (1982). Megatrends. New York: Warner Books.

National Commission for Excellence in Education. (1983). *A Nation at Risk: The Imperative for Educational Reform*. Washington, DC: U.S. Government Printing Office.

Nicklin, J. L. (1995, January 27, 1995). The Hum of Corporate Buzzwords: Colleges Look to Businesses for Advice on Restructuring. *Chronicle of Higher Education*, pp. A33.

Pederson, R. (1992, September 23, 1992). The Perils of TQM for the Academy. *The Chronicle of Higher Education*, pp. B4.

Peters, T. J. (1992). *Liberation Management: Necessary Disorganization for the Nanosecond Nineties*. New York: Alfred

A. Knopf.

Pica, J. A. (1995). Telephone Call.

Pryor, L. S. (1989). Benchmarking: A Self-Improvement Strategy. *Journal of Business Strategy*, 28-31.

PSQR. (1994). "Benchmarking" Being Bandied Too Broadly, *Public Sector Quality Report* (pp. 4). Lakeville, MN.

Reimann, C. (1995). HEPROC Assessment Home Page. Http://pobox.com/~higher. education: R & R Publishers.

Reutter, B. (1995). National Conference on Continuous Quality Improvement. CQI- L@MR.NET: Auburn University.

Rhoades, G. (1995). Rethinking Restructuring in Universities. *The Journal of Higher Education Management*, 10(2), 17-30.

Rudolph, F. (1977). *Curriculum: A History of the American Undergraduate Course of Study Since 1636*. San Francisco: Jossey-Bass.

Rush, S. C. (1994). Benchmarking—How Good is Good? In J. W. Meyerson & W. F. Massey (Eds.), *Measuring Institutional Performance in Higher Education* (pp. 83-97). Princeton: Peterson's.

Ryan, E. (1990). The Costs of Raising a Dollar. *Currents, 16*(8), 58-62.

Sandmeyer, L. (1995). Benchmarking on Campuses (pp. 4). HEP-ROC CQI-L Archive: American Association for Higher Education.

Sapp, M. M., & Temares, M. L. (1992). A Monthly Checkup: Key Success Indices Track Health of the University of Miami. *NACUBO business officer: magazine of the National Association of College and University Business Officers, 25*(9), pp. 24-31.

Schnell, G. (1995). Success Stories (with contacts) for CQI in Higher Education (pp. 6). HEPROC CQI-L Archive: American Association for Higher Education.

Sergiovanni, T. (1995). *Education Week*.

Seymour, D. and assoc., (Eds.). (1996). *High Performing Colleges: The Malcolm Baldrige National Quality Award as a Framework for Improving Higher Education* (Vols. 1-2). Maryville, MO: Prescott Publishing.

Seymour, D. (1994a, January/February). The Baldrige Cometh. *Change, 26*, 16-27.

Seymour, D. (1994b). Total Quality Management On Campus: Is It Worth It? *New Directions For Higher Education, 86*, 1-3.

Seymour, D. T. (1992). *On Q: Causing Quality in Higher Education*. New York: Macmillan Publishing. Company.

Shafer, B. S., & Coate, L. E. (1992). Benchmarking in Higher Education: A Tool for Improving Quality and Reducing Cost.

Business Officer, 26(5), 28-35.

Shaw, G. (1995). Benchmarking on Campuses (pp. 6). HEPROC CQI-L Archive: American Association for Higher Education.

Sherr, L. A., & Lozier, G. G. (1991). Total Quality Management in Higher Education. *New Directions For Institutional Research, 71,* 3-12.

Sill, D. (1995). Benchmarking II: What to Avoid at the State Level (pp. 7): HEPROC CQI-L Archive.

Sork, T. J., & Caffarella, R. S. (1990). Planning Programs For Adults. In B. B. Meriam & P. M. Cunningham (Eds.), *Handbook of Adult and Continuing Education* (pp. 233-245). San Francisco: Jossey-Bass.

Spendolini, M. J. (1992). *The Benchmarking Book.* New York: AMACOM.

Stark B. (1995). Benchmarking: Wish Lists/Benchmarkability (p. 3). HEPROC CQI-L

Archive: American Association for Higher Education.

Stein, R. H. (1995). Restructuring Universities. *Journal of Higher Education Management, 10*(2).

Sundstrom, D. (1995). BPRREENG-L Digest 81. bprreeng-l@lists.acs.ohio-state.edu: Ohio State University.

TBC. (1995). Internet Link to Business "Secrets" (pp. 1). Bedford, UK: The Best Practice Club.

TBE. (1995). www.benchnet.com: The Benchmarking Exchange, Inc.

Thor, C. G. (1995). *Practical Benchmarking for Mutual Improvement.* (Vol. 10). Portland, Oregon: Productivity Press.

Toffler, A. (1980). *The Third Wave.* New York: Morrow.

Tortarolo, J. S., & Polakoff, P. L. (1995). Benchmarking Health & Disability Benefits in the Energy & Communications Industries. *Benefits Quarterly, 1st Quarter,* 38-45.

Trow, M. (1973). *Problems in the Transition from Elite to Mass to University Higher Education* (ED091983). Berkeley: Carnegie Commission on Higher Education.

Veysey, L. R. (1965). *The Emergence of the American University.* Chicago: The University of Chicago Press.

Watson, G. H. (1992). *The Benchmarking Workbook: Adapting Best Practices for Performance Improvement.* Portland, OR: Productivity Press.

Watson, G. H. (1993). *Strategic Benchmarking: How To Rate Your Company's Performance Against the World's Best.* New York: John Wiley and Sons.

Watwood, W. B. (1995, January 6, 1995). Quality Assessment of

Higher Education. *The Chronicle of Higher Education*, pp. B4.

Wilson, L. (1995). Telephone Conversation: American Productivity and Quality Center.

Wolverton, M. (1994). *A New Alliance: Continuous Quality and Classroom Effectiveness.* ASHE-ERIC Higher Education Report No. 6. Washington, DC: The George Washington University, School of Education and Human Development.

Zemsky, R., & Massy, W. F. (1995). Toward an Understanding of Our Current Predicaments. *Change, 27*(6), 41-49.

INDEX

A

AACSB. See American Assembly of Collegiate Schools of Business

Academe Today, 101

Academic Quality Consortium of American Association for Higher Education, 15

ACHE. See Association for Continuing Higher Education

"Adapt, don't Adopt," 26

AERA. See American Educational Research Association

Albin (1995), 69

Alcoa 9-step benchmarking process, 23

Alstete (1994)
>   information technology helping in monitoring performance, 7

American Assembly of Collegiate Schools of Business, 4, 43
>   workshop on benchmarking and Management Education, 37

American Association for Higher Education, 53

American Educational Research Association Listservs, 101

American Productivity and Quality Center, 20, 30
>   definition of terms by, 65-66
>   offer a variety of services to begin a benchmarking process, 71
>   research study on causes of benchmarking project failures, 84

American Society for Quality Control
>   development of benchmarking software by, 86

American Society for Training and Development
>   creation of Benchmarking Forum by, 13

American universities periods of transition, 1

analysis of data as third step in benchmarking, 22

APQC. See American Productivity and Quality Center

Arizona State University benchmarking, 4

AskERIC Virtual Library, 101

assessment as a topic in efficiency and public accountability, 7

Associated Colleges of Indiana, 48

Association for Continuing Higher Education, 30, 45
>   Competitive Benchmarking Study, 45-47
>   measured primarily administrative processes, 67

Association for Institutional Research, 4

ASTD. See American Society for Training and Development

AT&T benchmarking, 12
>   12-step benchmarking process, 23

B

Babson College
> benchmarking focused on business transactions process, 54-55

Baldrige National Quality Award, 14-16
> sparked creation of several state-level quality awards, 16
> 1995 education criteria item listing, 96

Barclay (1995) benchmarking software
> used in graduate business program, 87-88

Bardach, Ken, 92
> GMAC/EBI Benchmarking Project results, 45

Bateman (1994)
> on internal benchmarking involving management education, 55

Bell, Don
> GMAC/EBI Benchmarking Project results, 45

Belmont University's Quality Team Manual on Benchmarking
> seven points to consider before benchmarking of, 63

Benchmarking
> "...Academic Credit and Noncredit Continuing Education," 51
>
> Action Plan, 84-85
>
> appropriate only where can immediately improve the process, 36
>
> can't use to predict future, 35
>
> Code of Conduct, 97-99
>
> comparison of popularity with TQM, 6-7
>
> data driven, 20
>
> early American college tradition of, xi
>
> failures top four causes, 84-86
>
> Forum and employee training, 13
>
> learning experience and not a fad, 27
>
> means of promoting substantive change-oriented action, 91
>
> process models, 24
>
> purpose to investigate and document the best practices, 23
>
> requires experience in quality management, 91
>
> *The Search for Industry Best Practices That Lead to Superior Performance*, 10
>
> Software, 86-88
>
> source of new ideas, 11-12
>
> starting process for, 63-64
>
> success at Xerox, 12
>
> two approaches to, 33
>
> two important overall components or process groups, 23

Business Process Reengineering, 2

as natural result of benchmarking, 91-92

can restrict thinking to framework of already being done, 35-36

institutional pioneer in applying, 9

C

colleges and universities
        faculty supportive of reform movement, 7
        survive by continually comparing and improving, 93
Colorado State University
        highest interest in benchmarking at, 68-69
        on list of Universities to benchmark, 51
competitive or peer benchmarking, 29-30
        appropriate for low or medium performing organizations,
        63
Consortium Studies, 47-49
Continuous Quality Improvement, 2
        Listserv, 53, 101
Cornell (Ezra) vision no longer possible, 90
Cornell University on list of Universities to benchmark, 51
cost benchmarks gap analysis example, 77
Council for the Advancement and Support of Education, 40
CQI. See Continuous Quality Improvement
CQI-L. See Continuous Quality Improvement Listserv
critical success factors, 65
CSFs. See critical success factors
"Culture of Quality", 58

D
Dale (1995)
        graphically analyzed benchmarking reveals performance
        gaps, 78
        qualifications for benchmarking team members, 64
        reengineering is really the natural result of benchmarking,
        32
Dalhousie University future plans for benchmarking, 59-60
dantatsu used to define benchmarking, 10
data
        recommended questions to clarify result of analysis of, 80-81
        sharing consortium value, 48
Deming, W. Edwards
        advice of "Adapt, don't Adopt," 25-26
        concept of benchmarking is foreign to philosophy of, 36
        Shewart Cycle was fundamental method taught by, 21
Design Steering Committee
        of American Productivity and Quality Center, 20
Detrick, Glenn, 43
Dossey-Terrell (1995) benchmarking
        at University of Central Florida, 53

E

Eastman Kodak Company

Carnegie Mellon University campus renovation process aided by partnering with, 92

EBI. See Educational Benchmarking, Inc.

Educational Benchmarking, Inc., 30, 101-102

formed to conduct full study of business schools, 45

educational testing benchmarking, 4

educators normally only borrow practices from other schools, 14

employees as observers of other organizations, 74

employee training study by Benchmarking Forum, 13

Entin (1994)

greater student-centeredness as a result of quality efforts, 7

Eric national literature database as source of individual institution comparative studies, 52-53

Ernst & Young, 87

expenditures and gift income study as early benchmarking effort, 40

"External Comparisons Project Team," 57

F

final stage of first benchmarking iteration actions, 81-82

financial surplus

leaders have a lower ratio of staff to students, 47

ratio of noncredit programs offered by offices of continuing education, 46

Ford (1993)

benchmarking functioning and human resources training, 13-14

functional benchmarking, 30-31. See also operational benchmarking

Functional Benchmarks in Higher Education, 34

Fund for Improvement of Postsecondary Education, 48

functional networks formation, 83

G

Gaither (1995)

information technology helping in monitoring performance, 7

gap analysis of cost benchmarks example, 77

GCP. See General College Program

General College Program curriculum, 50

generic benchmarking, 31-33

most difficult to use but best for long-term use, 32

I

IBM

> benchmarking at, 12
>
> 5-step benchmarking process, 23

Illes (1995)

> highest interest at Brigham Young University in academic not administrative, benchmarking, 68

Illinois Board of Higher Education

> use of benchmarking for purposes outside its definition, 60-61

Independent Colleges and Universities of Indiana, Inc., 48

Individual Benchmarking Project, 50-59

industry benchmarking. See Functional Benchmarking

information technology use in monitoring performance and quality, 7

Inger (1993)

> educators normally only borrow practices from other schools, 14

innovation achievement, 37

institutional benchmarking partners identification, 71

Institution Performance Results of Baldrige Award definition, 96

institutions of higher learning need focus and specialization, 90

Internal Benchmarking, 28-29

International

> Academy for Quality, 87
>
> Benchmarking Clearinghouse, 97, 102
>
> Quality Study, 63

Iona College's campus in Yonkers, 3

Iowa State University on list of Universities to benchmark, 51

Ithaca College

> joined The Benchmarking Exchange to obtain partners, 71-72

J

Japanese hoshin plan definition, 83

John Hopkins University modeled on German university, xi

K

Kansas State University on list of Universities to benchmark, 51

Keller (1983)

> criticism of, 8
>
> predicted academic competition for resources, 4-5

Kerridge (1995)

concept of benchmarking is foreign to true Deming
philosophy, 36
key success indices used at University of Miami, 69-70
Kinni (1994)
lessons that consistently occur in benchmarking literature,
89

L

LearnerFirst's *Benchmarking* software, 86-87
learning outcomes definition, 83
Learning Resources Network, 49
Leibfried and McNair (1992)
benchmarking is analogous to human learning process,
19-20
LERN. See Learning Resources Network
lessons that consistently occur in benchmarking literature, 89
Lily Endowment, 48
L. L. Bean benchmarked by Xerox, 28, 30-31
local ownership crucial for success of a quality improvement
process, 61
longitudinal data questions
to ask in analysis of influence of external variables, 80-81

M

Malcolm Baldrige National Quality Award
Pilot Study at Northwest Missouri State University, 58
use as a template for continuous quality improvement, 58
Massey and Meyerson (1994)
output benchmarking for gift processing performance, 78
maximum effectiveness of benchmarking
when supported by senior level administrators and
conducted by department units that will use data, 69
MBNQA. See Malcolm Baldrige National Quality Award
Merck (Edwin J.) on value of benchmarking at Wheaton College, 92
metrics
critical that benchmarking partner use the same, 90
Miami University of Ohio
comparing effectiveness of student achievements with State
University of New York at Fredonia, 51
Michigan State University, 92
GMAC/EBI Benchmarking Project results at, 45
Michigan Technological University, 36
Microsoft Excel spreadsheet

benchmarking software provided on, 86

mission statement of the organization

as a good place to identify candidates for benchmarking, 67-68

modeling against certain standards to produce a desired result

as a definition of benchmarking, xi

Motorola University

often does a better job of assessing the training and education

needs of their people than higher education does, 43

N

NACUBO. See National Association of College and University Business Officers

National Association of College and University Business Officers

Benchmarking Process for Improvement in Higher Education, 102

Benchmarking Project intended to cut costs rather than justify more dollars, 41

National Benchmarking Survey functional areas, 67

Project, 39-43

study, 29

National Conference on Continuous Quality, 4

National Cooperative Data Share - Benchmark Data Exchange, 48, 102

subscription service function, 48-49

National Institute of Standards and Technology Baldrige office, 15

negative performance gap definition, 75

New Course Cancellation Rates, 49-50

"new paradigm" requires building efficiency into the basic structure of the organization, 92

noncredit programs of continuing education offices benchmark, 46

North Carolina State University on list to benchmark, 51

Northwest Missouri State University, 58

1995 Education Pilot award criteria at, 16

most thorough institutional benchmarking application in higher education, 59

O

Oklahoma State University on list of Universities to benchmark, 51

operational benchmarking. See also functional benchmarking

functioning of, 33-34

value of, 34

Oregon State University

    institutional pioneer in applying total quality management, 9

    president of university identified principal customers and services to be provided to each customer group, 69

    questions to be asked when contacting another organization, 75

    state-mandated improvements involving benchmarking at, 61-62

    study of, 51-52

organizational weaknesses exposure minimized in benchmarking, 38

original research as a source for benchmarking data, 74

outcomes

    majority of process improvements involve one or more, 82-83

outcome assessment through benchmarking, 60

"out of the box" benchmarking as an opportunity to think, 10

output benchmarking example for gift processing performance, 78

outright copying of a business process

    without analysis for organizational fit can cause problems, 26

P

Pareto Principle

    20 percent of all activity affects 80 percent of the results, 65

parity performance gap definition, 75

PDCA. See Plan-Do-Check-Act

Pedersen (1992) questioned applicability of all recent quality improvement techniques to higher education, 36

Pennsylvania State University benchmarking, 53-54

performance gaps types description and consequences, 75-76

performance indicators

    as a topic in efficiency and public accountability, 7

    difference from benchmarking, 19

performance standards not the same as benchmarking, 19

Pica (Joe), 43

plagiarism and industrial espionage avoidance, 37

Plan-Do-Check-Act approach, 21

planning

    as first step in benchmarking, 22

    the benchmarking study, 23

positive performance gap definition, 75-76

post-industrial society as an information society, 1-2

post-secondary level of education as focus of quality improvement, 5

P-Q-P. See Priority-Quality-Productivity

"practical benchmarking." See operational benchmarking

Principle of Completion, 99

Principle of Confidentiality, 98

Principle of Exchange, 98

Principle of First-Party Contact, 98

Principle of Legality, 97

Principle of Preparation, 99

Principle of Third-Party Contact, 98-99

Principle of Understanding and Action, 99

Principle of Use, 98

Priority-Quality-Productivity, 61

process enablers

      fourth step in benchmark process, 22

      key to improving performance, 22

      need to identify, 81

      suggested creation of an action plan for implementation, 83

process "owner" function, 83-84

productivity

      as a topic in efficiency and public accountability, 7

      benchmarking as a means to measure, 4

      primary rational constraint on improvement is lack of availability for related data, 5

product/process improvement outcomes definition, 83

public domain information as source for benchmarking data, 74

Public University Data Sharing Consortium, 48

Q

quality efforts results, 7

quality movement in higher education reviewed in publications, 5

Quality Team Manual on Benchmarking

      seven points to consider before benchmarking, 63

Queensland University of Technology benchmarking study , 57

R

"Ratios for Success," 49

recycling or recalibration necessary for benchmarking process to be fully effective, 83

reengineering

      is the natural result of benchmarking, 32

      not proper tool for minor adjustments, 32

decreasing use in Boston area colleges, 7

and benchmarking comparison of popularity, 6-7

TQM

    See also Total Quality Management

Trow (1973)

    university management procedures become more dependent on quantified data for assessment of costs and benefits, 88

U

Ulrich benchmarking study of human resources practice, 13-14

"universal higher education" requires quantified data for assessment of costs and benefits, 88

University of Central Florida

    practices benchmarked with other organizations, 53

University of Chicago Graduate School of Business, 37, 55

University of Delaware

    internal benchmarking-like study, 50

    National Study of Institutional Costs and Productivity, 48

University of Hawaii benchmarking software used at, 87-88

University of Maryland

    benchmarking used successfully to reduce the processing time for surplus property requests, 55-56

University of Miami use of key success indices, 69-70

University of Michigan benchmarking study

    of human resources competencies and practice, 13-14

University of Minnesota GMAC/EBI Benchmarking Project

    identified significant internal problems and indicated appropriate action, 45

University of Oregon

    compared with Oregon State University, 62

    highest interest in benchmarking at, 69

    on list of Universities to benchmark, 51

University of Wisconsin

    joined The Benchmarking Exchange to obtain partners, 71-72

University System of Georgia description of

    organizational structures and administrative practices, 51

Upsala College in New Jersey, 3

U.S. Department of Education Web Server, 103

V

vertical benchmarking functioning, 35

Veysey (1965)

>huge changes in American universities from 1860 to 1900, 1
vision to "found an institution where any person can find
>instruction in any study" no longer possible, 90

W

Washington State University on list to benchmark, 51
Watson (1992)

>questionnaire proposed for use in a study of original
>research, 74
>questions when contacting another organization, 74-75
>suggested creation of an action plan for implementing each
>>individual process enabler, 83

Watson (1993), 22

>definition of strategic benchmarking by, 90
>focus of improvement efforts should be on processes that
>have highest potential for "return on attention," 65
>how strategic benchmarking differs from operational
>>benchmarking, 33
>recommended questions to clarify results of data analysis,
>>80-81

Watson (1995) on how competitive benchmarking

>differs from process benchmarking, 29-30

Westinghouse benchmarking, 12
West Virginia University, 36
Wheaton College in Massachusetts used benchmarking data

>to ensure that TQM and Business Process Reengineering
>efforts address areas with greatest potential for
>improvement, 42
>with TQM and BPR, 92

Wolverton (1994)

>benchmarking is only based upon current information, 35
world class benchmarking
>only suitable for already high-performing organizations, 63

X

Xerox company benchmarking, 10, 12, 23, 28, 30-31

ASHE-ERIC HIGHER EDUCATION REPORTS

Since 1983, the Association for the Study of Higher Education (ASHE) and the Educational Resources Information Center (ERIC) Clearinghouse on Higher Education, a sponsored project of the Graduate School of Education and Human Development at The George Washington University, have cosponsored the ASHE-ERIC Higher Education Report series. The 1995 series is the twenty-fourth overall and the seventh to be published by the Graduate School of Education and Human Development at The George Washington University.

Each monograph is the definitive analysis of a tough higher education problem, based on thorough research of pertinent literature and institutional experiences. Topics are identified by a national survey. Noted practitioners and scholars are then commissioned to write the reports, with experts providing critical reviews of each manuscript before publication.

Eight monographs (10 before 1985) in the ASHE-ERIC Higher Education Report series are published each year and are available on individual and subscription bases. To order, use the order form on the last page of this book.

Qualified persons interested in writing a monograph for the ASHE-ERIC Higher Education Report series are invited to submit a proposal to the National Advisory Board. As the preeminent literature review and issue analysis series in higher education, the Higher Education Reports are guaranteed wide dissemination and national exposure for accepted candidates. Execution of a monograph requires at least a minimal familiarity with the ERIC database, including *Resources in Education* and the *Current Index to Journals in Education*. The objective of these reports is to bridge conventional wisdom with practical research. Prospective authors are strongly encouraged to call Dr. Fife at 800-773-3742.

For further information, write to
    ASHE-ERIC Higher Education Reports
    The George Washington University
    One Dupont Circle, Suite 630
    Washington, DC 20036
Or phone (202) 296-2597; toll free: 800-773-ERIC.

Write or call for a complete catalog.

ADVISORY BOARD

James Earl Davis
University of Delaware at Newark

Susan Frost
Emory University

Mildred Garcia
Montclair State College

James Hearn
University of Georgia

Bruce Anthony Jones
University of Pittsburgh

L. Jackson Newell
University of Utah

Carolyn Thompson
State University of New York-Buffalo

L. Jackson Newell
University of Utah

Steven G. Olswang
University of Washington

Sherry Sayles-Folks
Eastern Michigan University

Karl Schilling
Miami University

Charles Schroeder
University of Missouri

Lawrence A. Sherr
University of Kansas

Marilla D. Svinicki
University of Texas at Austin

David Sweet
OERI, U.S. Dept. of Education

Kathe Taylor
State of Washington Higher Education Coordinating Board

Donald H. Wulff
University of Washington

REVIEW PANEL

Charles Adams
University of Massachusetts-Amherst

Louis Albert
American Association for Higher Education

Richard Alfred
University of Michigan

Henry Lee Allen
University of Rochester

Philip G. Altbach
Boston College

Marilyn J. Amey
University of Kansas

Kristine L. Anderson
Florida Atlantic University

Karen D. Arnold
Boston College

Robert J. Barak
Iowa State Board of Regents

Alan Bayer
Virginia Polytechnic Institute and State University

John P. Bean
Indiana University-Bloomington

John M. Braxton
Peabody College, Vanderbilt University

Ellen M. Brier
Tennessee State University

Barbara E. Brittingham
The University of Rhode Island

Dennis Brown
University of Kansas

Peter McE. Buchanan
Council for Advancement and Support of Education

Patricia Carter
University of Michigan

John A. Centra
Syracuse University

Arthur W. Chickering
George Mason University

Darrel A. Clowes
Virginia Polytechnic Institute and State University

Deborah M. DiCroce
Piedmont Virginia Community College

Cynthia S. Dickens
Mississippi State University

Sarah M. Dinham
University of Arizona

Kenneth A. Feldman
State University of New York-Stony Brook

Dorothy E. Finnegan
The College of William & Mary

Mildred Garcia
Montclair State College

Rodolfo Z. Garcia
Commission on Institutions of Higher Education

Kenneth C. Green
University of Southern California

James Hearn
University of Georgia

Edward R. Hines
Illinois State University

Deborah Hunter
University of Vermont

Philo Hutcheson
Georgia State University

Bruce Anthony Jones
University of Pittsburgh

Elizabeth A. Jones
The Pennsylvania State University

Kathryn Kretschmer
University of Kansas

Marsha V. Krotseng
State College and University Systems of West Virginia

George D. Kuh
Indiana University-Bloomington

Daniel T. Layzell
University of Wisconsin System

Patrick G. Love
Kent State University

Cheryl D. Lovell
State Higher Education Executive Officers

Meredith Jane Ludwig
American Association of State Colleges and Universities

Dewayne Matthews
Western Interstate Commission for Higher Education

Mantha V. Mehallis
Florida Atlantic University

Toby Milton
Essex Community College

James R. Mingle
State Higher Education Executive Officers

John A. Muffo
Virginia Polytechnic Institute and State University

L. Jackson Newell
University of Utah

James C. Palmer
Illinois State University

Robert A. Rhoads
The Pennsylvania State University

G. Jeremiah Ryan
Harford Community College

Mary Ann Danowitz Sagaria
The Ohio State University

Daryl G. Smith
The Claremont Graduate School

William G. Tierney
University of Southern California

Susan B. Twombly
University of Kansas

Robert A. Walhaus
University of Illinois-Chicago

Harold Wechsler
University of Rochester

Elizabeth J. Whitt
University of Illinois-Chicago

Michael J. Worth
The George Washington University

RECENT TITLES

1995 ASHE-ERIC Higher Education Reports

1. Tenure, Promotion, and Reappointment: Legal and Administrative Implications
   Benjamin Baez and John A. Centra

2. Taking Teaching Seriously: Meeting the Challenge of Instructional Improvement
   Michael B. Paulsen and Kenneth A. Feldman

3. Empowering the Faculty: Mentoring Redirected and Renewed
   Gaye Luna and Deborah L. Cullen

4. Enhancing Student Learning: Intellectual, Social, and Emotional Integration
   Patrick G. Love and Anne Goodsell Love

1994 ASHE-ERIC Higher Education Reports

1. The Advisory Committee Advantage: Creating an Effective Strategy for Programmatic Improvement
   Lee Teitel

2. Collaborative Peer Review: The Role of Faculty in Improving College Teaching
   Larry Keig and Michael D. Waggoner

3. Prices, Productivity, and Investment: Assessing Financial Strategies in Higher Education
   Edward P. St. John

4. The Development Officer in Higher Education: Toward an Understanding of the Role
   Michael J. Worth and James W. Asp, II

5. The Promises and Pitfalls of Performance Indicators in Higher Education
   Gerald Gaither, Brian P. Nedwek, and John E. Neal

6. A New Alliance: Continuous Quality and Classroom Effectiveness
   Mimi Wolverton

7. Redesigning Higher Education: Producing Dramatic Gains in Student Learning
   Lion F. Gardiner

8. Student Learning Outside the Classroom: Transcending Artificial Boundaries
   George D. Kuh, Katie Branch Douglas, Jon P. Lund, and Jackie Ramin-Gyurnek

1993 ASHE-ERIC Higher Education Reports

1. The Department Chair: New Roles, Responsibilities, and Challenges
   Alan T. Seagren, John W. Creswell, and Daniel W. Wheeler

---

2. Sexual Harassment in Higher Education: From Conflict to Community
   Robert O. Riggs, Patricia H. Murrell, and Joann C. Cutting

3. Chicanos in Higher Education: Issues and Dilemmas for the 21st Century
   Adalberto Aguirre Jr. and Ruben O. Martinez

4. Academic Freedom in American Higher Education: Rights, Responsibilities, and Limitations
   Robert K. Poch

5. Making Sense of the Dollars: The Costs and Uses of Faculty Compensation
   Kathryn M. Moore and Marilyn J. Amey

6. Enhancing Promotion, Tenure, and Beyond: Faculty Socialization as a Cultural Process
   William C. Tierney and Robert A. Rhoads

7. New Perspectives for Student Affairs Professionals: Evolving Realities, Responsibilities, and Roles
   Peter H. Garland and Thomas W. Grace

8. Turning Teaching Into Learning: The Role of Student Responsibility in the Collegiate Experience
   Todd M. Davis and Patricia Hillman Murrell

1992 ASHE-ERIC Higher Education Reports

1. The Leadership Compass: Values and Ethics in Higher Education
   John R. Wilcox and Susan L. Ebbs

2. Preparing for a Global Community: Achieving an International Perspective in Higher Education
   Sarah M. Pickert

3. Quality: Transforming Postsecondary Education
   Ellen Earle Chaffee and Lawrence A. Sherr

4. Faculty Job Satisfaction: Women and Minorities in Peril
   Martha Wingard Tack and Carol Logan Patitu

5. Reconciling Rights and Responsibilities of Colleges and Students: Offensive Speech, Assembly, Drug Testing, and Safety
   Annette Gibbs

6. Creating Distinctiveness: Lessons from Uncommon Colleges and Universities
   Barbara K. Townsend, L. Jackson Newell, and Michael D. Wiese

7. Instituting Enduring Innovations: Achieving Continuity of Change in Higher Education
   Barbara K. Curry

8. Crossing Pedagogical Oceans: International Teaching Assistants in U.S. Undergraduate Education
   Rosslyn M. Smith, Patricia Byrd, Gayle L. Nelson, Ralph Pat Barrett, and Janet C. Constantinides

1991 ASHE-ERIC Higher Education Reports

1. Active Learning: Creating Excitement in the Classroom
   Charles C. Bonwell and James A. Eison

2. Realizing Gender Equality in Higher Education: The Need to Integrate Work/Family Issues
   Nancy Hensel

3. Academic Advising for Student Success: A System of Shared Responsibility
   Susan H. Frost

4. Cooperative Learning: Increasing College Faculty Instructional Productivity
   David W. Johnson, Roger T. Johnson, and Karl A. Smith

5. High School-College Partnerships: Conceptual Models, Programs, and Issues
   Arthur Richard Greenberg

6. Meeting the Mandate: Renewing the College and Departmental Curriculum
   William Toombs and William Tierney

7. Faculty Collaboration: Enhancing the Quality of Scholarship and Teaching
   Ann E. Austin and Roger G. Baldwin

8. Strategies and Consequences: Managing the Costs in Higher Education
   John S. Waggaman

ORDER FORM 95-5

Quantity   **Amount**

_____ Please begin my subscription to the 1996 *ASHE-ERIC Higher Education Reports* at $98.00, 31% off the cover price, starting with Report 1, 1995. Includes shipping. _____

_____ Please send a complete set of the 1995 *ASHE-ERIC Higher Education Reports* at $98.00, 31% off the cover price. Please add shipping charge below. _____

Individual reports are available at the following prices:
1993, 1994, 1995, and 1996, $18.00; 1988–1992, $17.00; 1980–1987, $15.00

SHIPPING CHARGES
For orders of more than 50 books, please call for shipping information.

	1st three books	Ea. addl. book
U.S., 48 Contiguous States		
Ground:	$3.75	$0.15
2nd Day*:	8.25	1.10
Next Day*:	18.00	1.60
Alaska & Hawaii (2nd Day Only)*:	13.25	1.40

U.S. Territories and Foreign Countries: Please call for shipping information.
*Order will be shipped within 24 hours of request.
All prices shown on this form are subject to change.

PLEASE SEND ME THE FOLLOWING REPORTS:

Quantity	Report No.	Year	Title	Amount

Please check one of the following:
☐ Check enclosed, payable to GWU-ERIC.
☐ Purchase order attached.
☐ Charge my credit card indicated below:
    ☐ Visa   ☐ MasterCard

Subtotal: _____
Shipping: _____
Total Due: _____

Expiration Date_____

Name_____

Title _____ E-mail _____

Institution _____

Address_____

City _____ State _____ Zip_____

Phone _____ Fax _____ Telex_____

Signature _____ Date_____

SEND ALL ORDERS TO: ASHE-ERIC Higher Education Reports
The George Washington University
One Dupont Cir., Ste. 630, Washington, DC 20036-1183
Phone: (202) 296-2597 • Toll-free: 800-773-ERIC